"Buy a copy for every coworker you interact with. It's that essential. The twelve GOATS alone are worth the cost of the book."

—Seth Godin,
author of *The Song of Significance*

"Your must-have roadmap for courageous conversations at work. Karin Hurt and David Dye give you the tools, techniques, and inspiration to turn stress and frustration into career-defining moments of leadership and innovation."

—Dorie Clark,
executive education faculty at Columbia Business School
and WSJ best-selling author of *The Long Game*

"You get better at conflict to make things better. It's a profound paradox. Every working relationship will have a moment when it breaks. This book helps you not just to get through it but to improve the way you work together."

—Michael Bungay Stanier,
author of *The Coaching Habit* and
How to Work with (Almost) Anyone

"Mastering conflict is a disruptor's superpower, and Karin Hurt and David Dye are your guides as to how. They promise twelve powerful go-to phrases on dealing with conflict but deliver an astounding three hundred. This isn't just a book I recommend; I'm keeping it within arm's reach. Exceptionally practical, potentially transformative. Wow!"

—Whitney Johnson,
CEO at Disruption Advisors, top 10 management thinker,
Thinkers50, WSJ best-selling author of *Disrupt Yourself*

"Karin Hurt and David Dye's new book beautifully provides what is missing in virtually all books on conflict and conflict management: they provide a plethora of very specific examples of how choosing and then using particular words and phrases can make a huge difference in being able to resolve any conflict situation with others at work. They provide readers with the most effective verbal and non-verbal tools for keeping their challenging conversations going and thus creating an engaging and sustained setting in which all persons are more likely to ask the key questions, actively listen to one another's different perspectives, and then propose creative solutions so everyone can get their most important needs met in the conflict situation."

—Ralph H. Kilmann, PhD,
author of *Mastering the Thomas-Kilmann Conflict Mode Instrument (TKI)* and coauthor of the TKI assessment tool

"Thank goodness. This book addresses questions people often want to ask but don't and gives answers and guidance that are practical and real. There's lots of researched-based data, which lends credibility. And there's also experience-based and proven processes and models that lend reality. Many times, data doesn't quite cross over from theory and aspiration to keeping it real! Big thanks to Karin Hurt and David Dye for a book that will help build skills and effectiveness."

—Gloria (Glo) Cotton,
strategic leadership coach, pro-inclusionist,
and collaborative author of *Lead from Within*

"*Powerful Phrases for Dealing with Workplace Conflict* is a fabulous resource for everyone who works with anyone. Why? Because no matter who you are or where you work, conflict happens—and Karin Hurt and David Dye want you to be prepared. (Psst: chapter 3 is worth the price of the book!)"

—Ken Blanchard,
coauthor of *The New One Minute Manager*
and *Simple Truths of Leadership*

POWERFUL PHRASES

FOR DEALING WITH

WORKPLACE CONFLICT

WHAT TO SAY NEXT TO DE-STRESS THE WORKDAY, BUILD COLLABORATION, AND CALM DIFFICULT CUSTOMERS

KARIN HURT & DAVID DYE

HarperCollins
LEADERSHIP

AN IMPRINT OF HarperCollins

Published by HarperCollins Leadership, an imprint of HarperCollins Focus LLC.

Any internet addresses, phone numbers, or company or product information printed in this book are offered as a resource and are not intended in any way to be or to imply an endorsement by HarperCollins Leadership, nor does HarperCollins Leadership vouch for the existence, content, or services of these sites, phone numbers, companies, or products beyond the life of this book.

ISBN 978-1-4002-4629-8 (eBook)
ISBN 978-1-4002-4627-4 (TP)

Library of Congress Control Number: 2023950714

Printed in the United States of America
24 25 26 27 28 LBC 5 4 3 2 1

FOR YOU.
Because your voice matters.

Contents

SECTION III

Rising Above

Tackling Tricky Workplace Situations

What to Say When . . .

SECTION IV

Managing Up When You're Feeling Down
How to Deal with Conflict with Your Boss

What Do You Say If Your Boss . . .

SECTION V

Communicating with Difficult People
The Art of Wooing the Weary and Winning the Whiny

How to Deal With . . .

Introduction

You can't avoid conflict.

When there are problems to solve and people who care (and there are so many things to care about), you'll face conflict. And if you want to have more success, influence, and joy in your work, you've got to navigate it well. But conflict is hard. You weren't born knowing the perfect words to say when you're angry, dealing with a jerk, or when someone calls your game-changing idea "stupid."

You probably didn't learn practical, productive approaches to conflict in school. And, if you're like most of us, you grew up watching role models sometimes really screw it up. You've had some conflicts not go so well yourself, and you don't like how that feels. We hate that feeling too.

That's the reason for this book: to give you practical communication techniques to successfully navigate conflict at work. And when you do, you'll get better results, build trust, have more influence, and collaborate better with your coworkers.

First, a Confession

When Tim, our publisher, called and said, "Hey, we need a book to help people deal with today's challenging and complex workplace conflicts. Want to write it?" our first reaction was, "Yeah, sure. Makes sense. We can do that."

After all, we've been traveling the world shoving all brands of "diaper genies" into overhead compartments of planes for nearly a decade. ("Don't worry, it's clean," we always assure the surprised flight attendant.) And we've spent many hours walking jet-lagged around the streets the night before a keynote asking, "Hast du einen windeleimer?" or "Yǒu mài niàobù tǒng de ma?" (Do you have a diaper pail for sale?)

If you're not familiar with these stink-containing contraptions, you take a stinky diaper, put it in the genie, give it a twist, and plastic envelops the diaper so tight it doesn't stink. But, of course, the stink is still there, which you know if you've ever had the pleasure of emptying one of those long plastic-wrapped bundles of joy.

We're big believers that with workplace conflict, if you can't smell it, you can't solve it. And while we think these contraptions are a great invention for parents and babies, metaphorical genies can derail your influence and impact and destroy trust. So, "Yes, let's do it" was our first answer.

But, when we thought more deeply about actually writing the book, we had to ditch our own metaphorical genie and ask ourselves hard questions. How good are *we* at navigating conflict at work? Are we really qualified to write this book? As a married couple writing books together and running an international leadership development firm in the turbulence of a global pandemic and beyond, we're in a constant dance of conflict and collaboration. A few examples from our conversations with one another:

"I know you really want to take on this new strategic project, but that's not in our plan. I've got a ton on my plate right now, and there's no way I can do all the things."

"Hey, don't you realize how much work went into this? How about a bit more appreciation?"

"Don't tell me it's a stupid idea! First of all, it's brilliant. And would you ever talk to anyone on our team that way? Maybe read your own book on *Courageous Cultures* and respond with regard the next time."

Of course, in our "workplace," the stakes of a mismanaged conflict are high. Disagreements and hurt feelings don't turn off just because it's time to go to bed.

Like you, we wish workplace conflict was easier.

And so, we said yes. Not because we do conflict perfectly all the time, but because we know how challenging conflict is and how important it is for you to have practical skills and tools to do this well.

Why Is Conflict Hard?

The problem starts in your head. Your brain makes conflict hard because it treats every conflict as life or death. These instincts help when staring down a bear (either hide, fight, team up, or pretend you're dead). But for workplace conflict, those responses just make a gnarly situation worse. And, if you're like most people, you hope other people get you and maybe even like you. You want to feel safe and included. But your brain's survival instincts and fear of rejection are a little extra in a conversation about how your hybrid team policies aren't working or that nasty mess in the breakroom microwave.

And yet, when it comes to navigating workplace conflict and fostering collaboration, the stakes are high for you, for us, and for the world we are all building for our children. In this turbulent changing world with its messy, imperfect humans, you can't always predict what you'll show up to, but you can always choose how you show up. This book gives you choices so you can be more confident, ditch the metaphorical "diaper genie," show up with curiosity, and have conversations that matter.

How to Use This Book

We almost cut this section because the simple answer is, "Read it and use it." But there are a few quick pointers that can help. If you feel skeptical about whether this book is for you, read Karin's favorite chapter, the "What Abouts" in chapter 2. After that, section II has everything you need to set yourself up for success with any workplace conflict, including how to surface the conversation everyone wants to avoid and our GOAT (greatest of all time) Powerful Phrases. If you've picked up this book because you're in an ACE (acute conflict emergency), the table of contents will direct you to where you can get some quick advice. Of course, once you've aced your ACE, you can go back and get the foundations.

And, because navigating workplace conflict for greater influence and impact isn't just something you read about, it's something you do, we've built a vault of *free* resources and tools you can download to make these conversations even easier: templates, job aids, bonus content, team conversation starters, a book group facilitator guide, and a deeper dive into the research that grounds this book. We encourage you to use (and share) these resources to support your journey.

www.ConflictPhrases.com

THE NEW WORLD OF WORK
Workplace Conflict According to the Research

1

What Makes Workplace Conflict So Challenging?

"Due to burnout, my ability to see the silver lining or think
   holistically has diminished."

—Female, 42, United States

What's Making Conflict Harder Right Now?

People have had conflict with one another since, well, there have been people. But to give you the most useful tools, we wanted to find out what's happening now. So, we created the World Workplace Conflict and Collaboration Survey (WWCCS) to ask people around the world whether they're experiencing more (or less) conflict at work, what's causing those changes, and the effects of workplace conflict. We also asked about significant conflicts they've experienced and what advice they would give their former self if faced with that conflict again. At the time of writing, we've heard from over five thousand people in more than forty-five countries and all fifty of the United States.

At the beginning of each chapter, you'll find a quote from a WWCCS respondent (and a few people we've met in our travels) that includes a bit of their story, or advice, or the results of conflict. And you're invited to the party: we would love if you would add your voice and share your story about workplace conflict. You'll find the survey, more about our research, and the workplace conflict experiences of people around the world in the Workplace Conflict and Collaboration Resource Center.

www.ConflictPhrases.com

More Conflict at Work

If it feels like you're experiencing more conflict at work over the past few years, you're not alone. Seventy percent of the people in our research say that they're experiencing the same or more conflict at work. And of the 30 percent who said they've experienced less conflict, most of this group say they have less conflict because they changed jobs, are working from home, or escaped challenging people. We'd bet that in a lot of these circumstances, those changes made it more peaceful for that individual, but the workplace didn't improve, nor did anyone get better at conflict. Let's look at what's fueling this conflict and making it more intense.

Why Is There More Conflict at Work?*

Overwhelm, burnout, understaffing	27%
Poor management practices	27%
Pandemic-related mental health, anxiety	21%
Less tolerance, understanding for others	20%
Less motivated workforce	20%
Turbulent economy	16%
Discrimination	15%

WWCCS participants identified up to three causes.

TIRED WORKERS IN AN UNCERTAIN ECONOMY

The pandemic sped up changes in the workforce. More than ever before, people want meaning in their work.[1] And work itself is changing. The survey results citing continued overwhelm, economic instability, lower levels of motivation, and poor management are symptoms of this upheaval. Larger organizations have people scattered across seven different time zones. In a world of remote work, many of these people have never met each other in person. If you're in a matrixed organization, it gets more complicated. Lines of responsibility can be fuzzy, and your priorities or incentives might clash with your coworkers' goals. But you need your coworkers' help to succeed at your job. That's a conflict cocktail.

Since the pandemic, many industries find it more challenging than ever to attract and keep talent. Employees in the education, healthcare, service, and hospitality industries say they're sick and tired of rude and hostile customers, students, and patients, grueling hours, and impossible demands. And customers complain about long waits, poor service, apathetic staff, and tip creep. Another potent conflict cocktail.

The pandemic-inspired shift to remote work and hybrid teams left many people longing for deeper human connection. And even for those who've returned to the office (or never left in-person work), a few years of social distancing left many of us feeling unmoored. Many organizations are still wrestling with the new reality of remote and hybrid workforces. Managers are relearning how to lead and support their teams. Teammates are figuring out how to build meaningful relationships and get work done. These rapid changes and missing human connections fuel conflict and make it harder to solve.

PANDEMIC-RELATED MENTAL HEALTH AND ANXIETY

As mask mandates, stay-at-home orders, and online-only schooling fade into the rearview mirror, it's easy to forget the pandemic's disruption on nearly every aspect of life. But the COVID-19 pandemic traumatized many people and left scars. The social isolation bruised our psyches. "Choosing our bubble" of people created "us" and "them" dynamics that politics and social media made worse. For many, the pandemic's hypervigilance, anxiety, and stress created lasting mental health challenges.[2] For others, the resentment of mandates and loss of personal freedoms created another kind of fear and anxiety.

Take the increase in anxiety, stress, and depression, mix in the loss of human relationships, and you get more workplace conflict. And it's more intense. In chapter 3 we'll look at why human connection is so important for navigating conflict. For now, it's enough to say that all the isolation and loneliness people experienced isn't helping.

LESS TOLERANCE OR INCLUSION

We were sad to read WWCCS comments about alarming discrimination and lack of tolerance or inclusion. For many, these trends are getting worse. The pandemic sped up social change and intensified social media impacts, igniting conflict between people and groups and even families. You can't keep that tension out of the workplace. Let's break this down a bit.

Rapid Social Change

When things change fast or change in big ways, people freak out. Rapid change, major change, and unexpected changes can all increase the likelihood and intensity of conflict.[3] The pandemic was certainly an "all of the above" with rapid, major, and unexpected change. But it also happened alongside several other major changes. Social justice movements reached new levels of unrest and action. Thankfully, as a result, many people and organizations around the world have increased their commitment to diversity, equity, inclusion, and belonging.

At the same time, we see other troubling changes: an increase in visible white nationalism,[4] and global warming with concurrent droughts, fires, and floods.[5] Incredible leaps in artificial intelligence threaten to completely upend certain industries and careers. Sudden, significant change often leaves people feeling confused, anxious, and uncertain. You can see the consequences at work. One such example is the Society for Human Resource Management's analysis of social change and conflict resolution: compared to previous years, 44 percent of HR professionals report intensified political volatility at work in 2020; in 2016, only 26 percent reported increased political volatility compared to prior elections.[6]

Social Media

Social media thrives on conflict. These companies make their money from advertising and so do everything they can to keep people interacting with their platforms. One of the easiest ways to get people to interact is to push their anger and outrage buttons. This is due to what journalist and author Johann Hari, in his best-selling book *Stolen Focus*, describes as a quirk of human behavior. "On average," he writes, "we will stare at something negative and outrageous for a lot longer than . . . something positive and calm." It's called negativity bias. Hari sums it up: "If it's more enraging, it's more engaging."

Consistent exposure to this version of reality changes people. If you "expose yourself for hours a day to the disconnected fragments of shrieking and fury that dominate social media, your thoughts will start to be shaped like that . . . [you're] less able to hear more tender and gentle thoughts."[7] Social media hurts many people's ability to hear nuance, assume the best, and have a friendly conversation with other human beings. And these trends bleed over into the workplace.

Voices of Experience

Besides the global survey, we've also read and talked with hundreds of business and thought leaders to ask them for their experiences and wisdom about workplace conflict. Throughout the book, you'll find some of these insights in sidebars like this one from accountability expert Nate Regier. He calls us to struggle "with," rather than "against," so our conflict creates and builds a better future.

Expert Insight: Nate Regier

Our experience working in thousands of interpersonal conflict situations shows that when conflict occurs, human beings spend energy struggling. The struggle seems to take one of two forms: we either struggle against or we struggle with. Struggling against is everywhere. It's in politics and religion. On the news. On social media.

Struggling with is a process of mutuality and creation. It's about seeing the solution as a two-way street, viewing the struggle as an opportunity for a win-win outcome, and adopting an attitude of shared responsibility for resolving the discrepancy between what we want and what we are experiencing.

—Nate Regier, PhD, CEO of Next Element and author of *Conflict without Casualties* and *Compassionate Accountability*

The Path Forward

We don't share these causes of conflict to discourage you. The point is to understand where the conflict comes from and why it's happening. When you consider your colleague might be dealing with a ton of unnerving change, it gets easier to show up with compassion and curiosity and look for meaningful solutions.

Nine percent of our WWCCS respondents said the reason they're experiencing less conflict at work is "improved communication." Well, that's a start. Well-intentioned, care-filled words make a difference. And 32 percent of respondents who report less conflict at work attribute the decrease to "improved communication." That's our hope for you too—more choices in your communication leading to improved relationships, less stress, and better results.

2

What Abouts
Frequent Concerns, Questions, and Why Old Approaches Don't Work

"Drink the vodka."

—Male, 60, Russia

At this point, you probably have a few "what about" questions on your mind. Let's start with some of the most frequently asked questions about conflict from participants in our training and keynote programs. If you have more, head to our Conflict and Collaboration Resource Center and drop us a note. If there's anything we want to encourage, it's speaking up and talking about your concerns.

Powerful Phrases, really? I'm skeptical. You can't script this stuff.

There are many guides out there that claim to offer you a script for an entire conversation. Which of course won't work because: human beings. Every workplace conflict has nuance. You can't know exactly what you'll show up to or what the other person will say next.

We also know how many times our clients have asked us to "please just give me the exact words I can use." And those words, many of them based on the "advice for myself" component of our research, work like magic—repeatedly, across industries, with people at all levels of the organization, all over the world. But these aren't conversation scripts. They're Powerful Phrases that open the door for a meaningful conversation.

So, you're right, in that there are almost no "perfect words" for every situation except maybe "thank you," "I apologize," and "do *not* put that up your nose" (an unusual Powerful Phrase that rarely works but must still be said. Or shouted. Usually after it's too late). Apart from those, it's what the words *do* that matter most—not the words themselves. What the words do is carry meaning, create change, and build relationships by opening the door to a meaningful conversation.

The Powerful Phrases you'll find in this book are words you *can* use exactly as written, if that's comfortable for you. We will also give you the reasons they work and the intent behind them. So, when they don't fit your personality or the situation exactly, you can adapt and find your own Powerful Phrase that carries the same meaning, creates the changes, and builds the relationship. (And when you do, we'd love to hear it. Please share it with us in the Resource Center.)

In chapter 3 you'll learn how to navigate the four dimensions common to most conflict conversations. As you read through any Powerful Phrase in this book, we invite you to consider how the other person might respond, and then how you can respond to guide the conversation through these four dimensions.

I'm so tired of "I" statements, sandwich methods, and that nonsense. It doesn't work.

There's a lot of traditional workplace communication wisdom that gets passed on but makes little sense—or just plain won't work in different scenarios. Most of these suggestions improved what came before and helped in their time. Unfortunately, time has stolen their power, and these old standbys are often punch lines (for good reason).

"I" statements and sandwich feedback are two examples. And if you're unfamiliar with these, don't worry. You won't find them here because they're too easily misunderstood and misused. But before we dismiss these two bits of feedback history, here's a quick look at where they came from and when they're useful.

First, the old-school "I" statement. This is where you don't talk about the other person. Instead, you focus on your experience, starting with an "I" statement. Something like, "I am frustrated, my team can't get our work done, and we can't get you the funding when we don't have your data."

The value of the "I" statement is that it focuses on your experience. And there's a ton of research that suggests starting a feedback conversation with your experience is a good idea.[1] The problem comes because most people just remember the "I" part of the statement and not the intent behind it. So, they say things like "I can't believe you're being such a jerk!"

Well, technically, that begins with "I"—but really, it's still about the other person. And then, when they try to fix it, the sentence contorts into something that would give your high school writing teacher nightmares: "I can't believe that you, uh, I mean, I feel like you're a big jerk. Wait. I want you to stop being such a jerk. Nope, that's not it. Ugh. Okay, how about I just want you to leave me alone, let me get my work done, and stop being such a jerk? Okay?"

The other feedback technique that people love to hate is called sandwich feedback. You've got something potentially difficult to say, so rather than just say it, you sandwich it. Good-bad-good.

People not-so-lovingly refer to this as a sh** sandwich. Great alliteration, but not so useful for meaningful conversations. The sandwich has two problems when you use it to start a conversation. First, your message gets lost. The person focuses on one compliment and misses the meaningful middle. The second problem is that the sandwich feels insincere and manipulative. "She said something nice. Great, what did I do wrong this time?"

Now, when someone *asks you* for your feedback, yes, reinforce something they're doing well and give them an idea to work on. Otherwise, save the sandwiches for lunch. We'll avoid the confusion and lost opportunities in these techniques and give you some easier ways to open the conversation in chapter 4.

My [boss/coworker/customer] is a psychopath. There's nothing I can do that's going to help.

Ouch. We're sorry to hear the situation is that bad. And you are not alone. We've heard so many stories of conflict with managers in the WWCCS. We want to encourage you to know that there is hope. Many times, we can talk ourselves into helplessness and feel like a victim of circumstances before we try having a conversation and asking for what we want.

It's easy to create stories about the other person and wonder how they could be so clueless, selfish, or inconsiderate, when really, they're just doing the best they can. Our conversation creates a chance for change. Nothing changes if you stay silent.

True, you can speak up and the circumstances might not change. But you still come out ahead in three ways. First, you have developed your skill and courage. Both improve with practice. The next time you need to have a conversation like this, you'll be more ready for it.

The second benefit is that you may learn something you didn't know. Maybe that person isn't inconsiderate. Maybe they have a competing set of priorities you didn't understand (and yes, there's a Powerful Phrase for that—see chapter 12). The third change when you learn nothing new, and circumstances don't change, is that now you have real data about your workplace and you learn that it may not be a good fit for you. Sometimes removing yourself is the best solution (see chapter 7 for more). Now you know.

Expert Insight: Liane Davey

Should you mind your own business when you see conflict on your team? In most cases, the answer is no. So, how can you justify poking your nose in?

First, if there is a conflict that is affecting your team or affecting your company, I would argue that it is your business. When your boss is unwilling to prioritize, it's you that must stretch yourself across too many projects. When your teammates are passive-aggressive, it's you who must deal with the unresolved issues and the inefficient work-arounds. When individuals fail to stand up for themselves, it's you who must listen to their pessimistic views on the world. The majority of conflict on your team becomes your business.

A second reason to ignore the "mind your own business" mantra is that you might actually be in a much better position to help with the conflict if you aren't directly involved.

I first started thinking about this when I heard parenting expert Barbara Coloroso talk about the Bully, the Bullied, and the Bystander. It's research that shows that bullying is a dynamic among three parties. We all wish the bully would behave differently and we hope the bullied will stand up for himself, but the person with the best chance to end bullying in the moment is the bystander.

The same is true in teams. I use different terms, but the idea is the same. There are certainly wicked people (or at least people who behave wickedly). There are also wounded people; the ones who feel victimized and are beyond doing anything to make the situation better. In these situations, it's the witness—the one with some emotional distance—who has the best chance to intervene constructively.

—Liane Davey, author of *The Good Fight: Use Productive Conflict to Get Your Team and Organization Back on Track*

I can't change an entire culture by myself—does everyone in my workplace need to read this to make it work?

Yes, everyone needs to read this book. Please contact us for bulk discounts.

Just kidding. Sort of.

While we would love everyone at work to read and use these Powerful Phrases, you can absolutely use them on your own, whether or not the other person knows them. We will walk you through the process of conflict conversations, give you the words to use, and explain the reasons to use them. These aren't hacks or manipulations. They always maintain the dignity and humanity of everyone involved. And yes, when the other person also knows these techniques, you'll both be able to work through meaningful conflict more quickly.

There are so many Powerful Phrases in this book. How can I possibly remember them all and use them when I need them?

Short answer: you can't remember them all (unless you're Italian Andrea Muzii, current World Memory Champion) and you don't need to. Use the book as a reference and plan your strategy. If you want to memorize a few Powerful Phrases, the twelve greatest of all time in chapter 3 will serve you well.

GETTING STARTED

Practical Approaches for
Every Workplace Conflict

3

Start Here

The Four Dimensions of Constructive Conflict

"Be the bigger person and talk about it."

—Nonbinary, 37, South Africa

W e've established that you can't script influence and we can't possibly give you a phrase for every single workplace conflict. But no matter what conflict you face, there will always be four dimensions that will make it productive. Every Powerful Phrase in this book addresses one of these dimensions. And, when you run into a challenging situation or coworker conflict that's not in the book, you can start with one of these four dimensions to figure out what to say next. Let's look at each one and how it shows up in your conflicts.

The Four Dimensions of Constructive Conflict

1. Connection—Do we know one another as human beings?
2. Clarity—Do we have a shared understanding of success?
3. Curiosity—Are we genuinely interested in other perspectives and what's possible?
4. Commitment—Do we have a clear agreement?

1. Connection—Do We Know One Another as Human Beings?

Workplace conflict always involves people—and every conflict gets easier the more you know one another, understand one another's perspectives, and see one another as human beings. Imagine that you're in a clash with a coworker named Joe. You've come together to talk about it. Joe opens the conversation with a Powerful Phrase: "I really care about you and this project, and I'm confident we can find a solution we can all work with."

Well, if Joe's basically a good guy, who got you out of a bind last year when your little boy was sick . . . and, oh yeah, just last week he told your boss you're a rock star at pivot tables (that sure was nice of him), that's a solid way for Joe to start the conversation. You might think, "Well, I'm frustrated, but come to think of it, Joe always seems fair. Let me listen to what he has to say. He's right. I bet we can work this out."

Now imagine the same conflict, different Joe. This Joe recently threw you under the bus and took credit for your work. Oh yeah, and last week he laughed at your idea during the staff meeting. In front of your boss and all the people. Now, if Joe starts the conversation the same way, by saying, "I really care about you and this project . . ." you might think, "Nice try, Joe, but that's a hard stop. I don't trust you."

That's the power of connection. The more connection you can build before you need it, the easier conflict becomes. And yeah, for many people, connection feels challenging right now because of lingering pandemic hangover, hybrid or remote work, and cross–time zone teams. As you seed the ground for easier collaboration, influence, and trust, one of the best things you can do is get to know the people you work with as people, not just their function. Treat them with dignity and be trustworthy. It takes extra time, but you'll earn it back many times over when you work through conflict. If you've not invested in the relationship, or the other person doesn't trust your intentions, even the most carefully chosen words will fall flat.

And speaking of connection—there's one more person to connect with: you. Constructive conflict requires you to know your values, your goals, what you need, and what you want. You'll see several connection Powerful Phrases throughout the book that ask you to connect to yourself.

2. Clarity—Do We Have a Shared Understanding of Success?

Think about any significant conflict you have now or had in the past. We're willing to bet that the source of that conflict includes an expectation violation. You thought they'd clean up their coffee mugs after the meeting. They thought the magic coffee mug fairy would take care of it. Everyone carries around expectations of one another. And sometimes, you don't even know you have an expectation until someone doesn't live up to it. So, the second dimension of constructive conflict is to get on the same page: create clarity about outcomes and expectations.

One of the common mistakes we see people make in workplace conflict is that they don't clearly understand what success looks like. So, you get conversations like this:

Jack: "I don't like this."
Jill: "Okay, what would you like to see happen?"
Jack: "I don't know. I'm not sure what I want."

Can you feel the frustration? That's a conversation that can't go anywhere. (And before you feel bad when you show up like Jack . . . listen, we do it too.)

When you get clear for yourself and help other people find their clarity, *now* you can have a more productive conflict conversation.

3. Curiosity—Are We Genuinely Interested in Other Perspectives and What's Possible?

One of the fastest ways to get to the root cause of a workplace conflict is to show up genuinely curious about the other person's perspective. Your sincere curiosity helps people feel seen and gives you a better understanding of what it will take to solve a problem.

This is often the hardest part of constructive conflict because you have your point of view for a reason. It's hard to be curious when you feel angry or disrespected. And yet . . . the cool thing about curiosity is that when you ask a good question, it automatically helps pull you out of that reactivity. It's hard to be angry and genuinely curious at the same time.

Now you might think, "Oh, I'm curious all right. I want to know, 'What's wrong with them? How can they be so freakin' stupid?'" Those are questions, of course, but they are extensions of your frustration and won't help you understand the other person's point of view. And that's why we specify *good* questions. Questions that increase understanding. That help you build on another's ideas. Questions with answers that make you say, "Huh, you know, I never thought of it that way." And we'll give you plenty of these effective curiosity questions throughout the book.

4. Commitment—Do We Have a Clear Agreement?

One of the most frustrating aspects of workplace conflict conversations is that it seems like they'll never end. As you connect, get curious, and build on one another's suggestions, your conversation needs to produce action, or nothing changes. And if nothing changes, it's *worse* than if you never had a conversation. Now you've wasted time, trust drips away, and people lose hope. Commitment is the answer and the key to move you from words to action.

There are two keys to a useful commitment. The first is to get specific. You want specific actions with specific owners who have specific finish lines. The second key to an effective commitment is to schedule a time to review your agreement. Let's look at an example.

Say you have a peer you rely on for data, let's call him Don. And the two of you are in conflict because Don's not giving you the reports you need for your team members to do their jobs. You have a friendly conversation, and because Don's team is drowning in work, you agree your team will request the data only once a week.

That's good so far, but that's not a commitment. You still need specific actions, specific owners, and specific finish lines, with a specific time to review your commitment. So, you build the following agreement: This Friday, you will explain the new process to your team. Your team members will get data requests to Don's team by 3:00 p.m. on Tuesday. Don will explain the new process to his team at their meeting tomorrow morning. Don's team will supply the requested data on Wednesdays by noon. You and Don will meet in two weeks on Monday at 4:30 p.m. to see how it's going.

The specificity makes it clear what everyone will do. You don't leave it up to good intentions. The follow-up meeting makes it more likely that you will both keep your commitments, and it creates time to deal with the inevitable challenges that will disrupt your new plan.

The Greatest of All Time (GOAT) Powerful Phrases

Now, you might be thinking, "Okay: Connection, Clarity, Curiosity, and Commitment, I get it. They're important. But how do you do these in the middle of a conflict?" That's a good question. We've got you.

Enter Powerful Phrases. Throughout the book, you'll get specific phrases that will help build connection, establish clarity, cultivate curiosity, and create commitments in many specific conflict scenarios. But what if you had go-to Powerful Phrases that you could use in almost any situation? That would be helpful, right? We've chosen twelve go-to, all-purpose Powerful Phrases that are the GOAT (greatest of all time) because you can use them in many different conflict conversations. There are three for each of the dimensions of constructive conflict.

The Twelve Greatest of All Time Powerful Phrases for Dealing with Workplace Conflict

CONNECTION

1. "I care about (you, this team, this project) and I'm confident we can find a solution we can all work with."

2. "Tell me more."

3. "It sounds like you're feeling ___, is that right?"

CLARITY

4. "What would a successful outcome do for you?"

5. "Let's start with what we agree on."

6. "What I'm hearing you say is _____. Do I have that right?"

CURIOSITY

7. "I'm curious how this looks from your perspective?"

8. "What do you suggest we do next?"

9. "What can I do to support you right now?"

COMMITMENT

10. "What's one action we can both agree to as a next step?"

11. "To recap, we've agreed to ___. Is that your understanding?

12. "Let's schedule time to talk about this again and see how our solution is working."

CONNECTION

These phrases help you start a human-centered conversation:

1. "I care about _____ (you, this team, this project) and I'm confident we can find a solution that we can all work with."

Acknowledge the challenge, your difference of opinions, and your confidence that you can work through it together. If your past behavior makes this statement questionable, you'll want to add a sincere apology as you state your intent for your future relationship.

2. "Tell me more."

Nothing builds connection like being seen, and this Powerful Phrase gets there in just three words. See the sidebar for more.

Expert Insight: Justin Jones-Fosu

"Tell me more."

These three words provide context and help you better understand what people are saying—and what they mean by what they say. When we don't understand context, we make our own conclusions. That is catastrophic.

"Tell me more" helps you listen deeply and lessens the chance of conflicts based on misunderstandings. In a conflict conversation or a conversation with people who differ from you, you can use this kind of follow-up question once or twice to get past the surface question and into what's real for that other person.

—Justin Jones-Fosu, CEO of Work. Meaningful. and author of *The Inclusive Mindset: How to Cultivate Diversity in Your Everyday Life*

3. "It sounds like you're feeling _____. Is that right? [pause for affirmation]. Thank you for letting me know how you feel."

This Powerful Phrase is a tried-and-true relationship-building technique called "reflect to connect." When you "reflect to connect," you're not agreeing with what they've said or telling them you agree with their emotion. Rather, you're acknowledging how they feel. You see them. When you reflect, you create a common starting place for the conversation.

When they know you've seen and heard them, it diffuses some of the emotional intensity and builds a connection that allows you to move to constructive next steps. Checking in with the other person to validate their feelings can also help de-escalate a conflict at any point in the conversation.

Here's an example of this one in use: "It sounds like you're really frustrated with the lack of response from marketing and that's draining your motivation. Do I have that right?"

CLARITY

Use these GOATs to uncover expectations and create clarity:

4. "What would a successful outcome do for you?"

You may or may not agree on what success looks like, but gaining clarity around expectations can save a lot of time and wasted energy. If it turns out you both want the same thing, you can shift to a "how can we" conversation: "Great, it sounds like we both want something similar. So how can we make that happen?"

At the very least, this powerful question gives you insights into what the other person needs and opens the door for you to share your definition of success.

5. "Let's start with what we agree on."

When you're in the middle of a workplace conflict, it's easy to overlook the common ground. It's likely you share some common perspective to build on. Taking a few minutes to know where you agree can help reduce stress and create a more collaborative tone for the work ahead.

6. "What I'm hearing you say is _____. Do I have that right?"

This is a check for understanding to show that you're actively listening, interested in, and truly see the other person's point of view. This Powerful Phrase is gold when working through workplace conflict because it also helps clear up misinterpretations and misunderstandings.

CURIOSITY

These three Powerful Phrases are curiosity GOATs because they get you out of your frustration, help you genuinely find out what's happening for the other person, and open up possibilities:

7. "I'm curious how this looks from your perspective."

The beauty of this Powerful Phrase is that it can be useful at almost any point in the conversation. Variations include "What's your take on this situation?" and "I'd love to hear your point of view on this." Of course, once you listen to their perspective, you set the stage to share yours.

8. "What do you suggest we do next?"

This Powerful Phrase can be so useful to move the conversation from complaining or hand-wringing to tangible next steps, and it sets you up to share your ideas as well.

9. "What can I do to support you right now?"

This question is an excellent follow-up to the curiosity questions. One of the fastest ways to de-escalate an emotional conversation is to show up with genuine curiosity about how you might help.

As you get curious and look for solutions, build on one another's ideas. You will probably find new ways of approaching the issue that neither of you had considered. Then you can evaluate these solutions against your shared understanding of success. Get curious again—do these ideas achieve your mutual outcomes? Or do you need some more ideas? Can you modify one of these ideas to get there?

COMMITMENT

These next three GOATs will help you move your conflict conversations to specific commitments:

10. "What's one action we can both agree to as a next step?"

You might not have resolved all the issues, but steering the conversation to one specific next step builds momentum. Asking for just one action will usually feel doable. And if one step feels easy, you can always say, "Great, what else do you think we could do?"

11. "So, to recap our conversation, we've agreed to _____. Is that your understanding?"

We're big believers in the "check for understanding" throughout the conversation. It's so valuable when recapping a workplace conflict conversation. The more emotionally intense the conversation, the more critical this final step is. If you leave the discussion with different expectations, you'll have continued conflict and hurt feelings. And this final Powerful Phrase can make all the difference between a pleasant conversation and a conversation that creates lasting change.

12. "Let's schedule some time to talk about this again and see how our solution is working."

If you've ever been in one of our leadership training programs, you'll recognize this as "scheduling the finish." One major source of workplace conflict is when you think you've resolved it, and everything doesn't go the way you planned. Scheduling time to talk about the situation again makes the follow-up conversation more natural because you've already agreed to it. A scheduled follow-up increases the odds that you'll both keep your commitments to one another. And it gives you a built-in opportunity to discuss the inevitable disruptions to your plan.

These twelve GOAT Powerful Phrases give you a great start for any conflict. In the following chapters, we'll provide you with additional ideas for what to say in more nuanced and specific conflicts.

Visit the Resource Center for a printable job-aid with all twelve GOAT Powerful Phrases for Dealing with Workplace Conflict.

www.ConflictPhrases.com

The Twelve GOAT Powerful Phrases for Workplace Conflict

CONNECTION

1. "I care about _____ (you, this team, this project) and I'm confident we can find a solution that we can all work with."
2. "Tell me more."
3. "It sounds like you're feeling _____. Is that right? [pause for affirmation]. Thank you for letting me know how you feel."

CLARITY

4. "What would a successful outcome do for you?"
5. "Let's start with what we agree on."
6. "What I'm hearing you say is _____. Do I have that right?"

CURIOSITY

7. "I'm curious how this looks from your perspective."
8. "What do you suggest we do next?"
9. "What can I do to support you right now?"

COMMITMENT

10. "What's one action we can both agree to as a next step?"
11. "So, to recap our conversation, we've agreed to _____. Is that your understanding?"
12. "Let's schedule some time to talk about this again and see how our solution is working."

4

Courage Matters
Get More Confidence to Start the Conversation Everyone Wants to Avoid

"As a young manager, having not done well at leading, my team approached me and addressed what they saw needed to change. We had a respectful and open conversation about our needs and agreed what each party needed to change. From there on the collaboration changed completely—not to perfect—but to very good. I am still grateful that they decided to trust me and be open about how they saw the situation!"

—Male, 58, Denmark

N ow that you're familiar with the GOAT Powerful Phrases, let's talk about how to get into a productive conflict conversation. Now, you might be thinking, "Wait, what? Start the conversation . . . like, uncover it, bring it up, actively make conflict happen? That's the last thing I want to do." We hear you.

It's so tempting to ignore conflict at work. After all, it takes courage and energy to start the conversation. That's why so many people go for the diaper genie. Sometimes it just feels easier to pretend everything's good, avoid the negativity, keep the conversation light, and wait until you get home to vent to your dog (cats are notoriously unhelpful for venting and the humans in your life will tire of it).

Most Common Negative Effects of Workplace Conflict*	
Stress	54%
Employees leave	33%
Lower quality of work	31%
Reduced productivity	30%
Absenteeism	20%
Disengagement/quiet quitting	19%
Less innovation or creativity	17%

*WWCCS participants identified up to three effects of workplace conflict.

Here's the thing: conflict is like fire or water. Both elements can help or harm. Destructive conflict can obliterate everything in its path; it tears people down and has no true "winner." Just look at the top consequence of conflict from the WWCCS: stress, turnover, lower-quality work, lost productivity. No one needs more of that in their life. These are the consequences of destructive conflict.

But productive conflict focuses on ideas and dignity. It helps you and others get smarter, as you broaden perspectives and consider alternative points of view. And while many more people in the WWCCS mentioned the negative effects of workplace conflict, we also saw positive outcomes when people had the skills to navigate conflict productively. Improved quality of work, positive policy changes, and more innovation all

result from productive conflict. So how do you get more confidence to start a productive conflict conversation?

**Most Common Positive Effects of
Workplace Conflict***

Improved quality of work	12%
Positive policy change	10%
More innovation or creativity	8%

**WWCCS participants identified the top
three effects of workplace conflict.*

When Silence Is Selfish

Early in my (David's) career, our CEO planned to run a
major marketing event that I felt lacked integrity. I lost sleep
over it, wondering how my CEO could act that way. It gnawed
at me, and my stomach churned with frustration. At first, I
said nothing because . . . CEO, right? But I reached a point
where I couldn't take it anymore. The conflict in my head
caused me so much grief that I had to do something. Finally,
I spoke up. I met with our CEO and told him I couldn't take
part in the event because I believed his approach lacked
integrity.

What do you think happened next?

We often imagine the worst outcomes. When we avoid conflict, it's because we're focused on the destructive possibilities.
But what happened this time surprised me. The CEO said,
"David, I see it differently and, no, I don't think there's an
integrity problem. But I also don't want you to do something

that's out of conscience for you. What can we do that would make the event feel in integrity for you?"

As I thought about it, I realized there was an easy fix for the situation that would help the CEO achieve his marketing goals and keep us in total integrity. I made my suggestion, and he said, "Great, let's do that." The event went well, I had more peace of mind, and I even got a reputation as a values-based leader.

When you speak up about something that's bothering you, it's not destructive. You're giving everyone else (and you) a chance to learn, grow, and respond. Silence is selfish in these moments because it steals their opportunity to be better.

Beyond giving everyone a chance to grow, getting good at conflict will also bring you peace of mind, and less stress, and help you make better decisions, improve trust, and give you more influence. Get the confidence to start the conversation by focusing on all those positive outcomes, and the negative outcomes if you do nothing.

And yeah, sometimes you'll speak up and you won't get through. If the CEO had a different, "shut up and do as I say" reaction, I would have had more information and a different choice to make. You'll get more about what to do when your words don't work in chapter 7.

Similar to ditching the "diaper genie," one of our favorite clients in Switzerland tells us, "Sometimes you just have to *put the fish on the table* and talk about what stinks." We're confident that your courage to open the dialogue will pay off. Here are a few conversation starters, beginning with the conversation to have with yourself.

Powerful Phrases to Ask Yourself and Build Your Confidence

"What do I want to happen because of what I say?"

This one might seem obvious, but conflict can be messy. You might want to say all the things. When summoning the courage to surface conflict, one of the best things you can do is know why you want to have the conversation.

Get clear on your intention. Consider what you want the other person to think, feel, or do because of your conversation.

Expert Insight: Jeff Hayes

The Myers-Briggs Company's recent research on conflict[1] found a significant relationship between the ability to manage conflict and job satisfaction. Specifically, those with the most positive view on their ability to manage conflict also tended to have higher levels of job satisfaction, felt more able to be their authentic self at work, and felt more valued by and at home in their organizations. Conflict happens at all levels of organizations (and in everyone's personal life at some level). Being better able to manage and navigate conflict sooner and more effectively means that you will feel more satisfied and be more confident to face the next conflict challenge that comes your way.

—Jeff Hayes, president and CEO, Myers-Briggs Company

"Why does what I have to say matter?"

Bernard Meltzer hosted a popular radio call-in show called *What's Your Problem?* He summarized sage advice from many wisdom traditions this way: "Before you speak, ask yourself if what you are going to say is true, is kind, is necessary, is helpful. If the answer is no, maybe what you are about to say should be left unsaid."

That's a good filter as you consider whether to start the conversation. If what you have to say is true, kind, necessary, and helpful, then it matters. Connect with that "why."

"What's preventing me from saying it?"

This is where you get in touch with your own fears and the story you're telling yourself about what might happen. Are you concerned about "last times"? Are you worried about the relationship? Understanding what's holding you back can help form your message.

"What's at stake if I stay silent?"

Dr. Amy Edmondson, the pioneer of psychological safety, often talks about how people are more likely to discount the future benefits of speaking up and overweight their current fear.[2] When you ask yourself this powerful question, you consider the future and the risks of staying silent.

Martin Sheen shares this poignant Irish tale to emphasize that standing up for what you believe comes at a cost—but that it's worth it:[3]

A man arrives at the gates of heaven and asks to be let in. St. Peter says, "Of course, just show us your scars."

The man says, "I have no scars."

St. Peter replies, "What a pity. Was there nothing worth fighting for?"

When you're nervous about starting the conversation, consider the long view. Are you the kind of person who cares enough to try?

"What's the worst that can happen here?"

This Powerful Phrase can be strangely empowering. One of our clients, a US Marine veteran, is fond of saying, "When I get too stressed about a workplace conflict, I just remember, *no one is shooting at me.*" The worst that can happen is usually nowhere near as bad as your imagination suggests.

Powerful Phrases to Invite Others into the Conversation

After connecting with your intention, it's time to start the conversation. Here are some phrases to begin the conversation with curiosity:

"I'm concerned that we might not be talking about _____. And my hunch is that's because of _____. Here's why I think we need to have the conversation anyway. What do you think?"

This technique can help get a conversation started when you don't know for sure what's causing the silence, but you have a hunch. You open with a conversation about the conversation. By providing a possible answer, you make it safer for people to respond.

Here are three variations you can use in different circumstances:

- "What's one issue we're not talking about that would make all the difference in our effectiveness?"
- "I'm sensing that there's something important we're not talking about. Do you feel that way too?"
- "I care too much about our relationship to not talk about this."

If you sense your conflict might be due to unspoken fears and misaligned expectations, these next two Powerful Phrases are sets of questions you can use to help everyone know what others feel and think. They can lead to incredibly powerful discussions.

"What are your biggest hopes for this project?" and "What are your biggest fears?"

"In the next six months, what are you most looking forward to and what are your biggest concerns?"

These questions are powerful when forming a new team, starting a new project, or embarking on any new initiative. As people share their answers, the discussion builds connection and an opportunity to solve problems early. It's amazing how eager people are to share what's on their hearts and minds. You can easily surface the conversations that need to happen and discuss tangible solutions.

Finding the courage to start an uncomfortable conversation can be tricky, but when you connect with yourself and invite people into conversation, you'll save everyone from future headaches and heartaches.

Powerful Phrases to Surface Conflict and Start the Conversation Everyone Wants to Avoid Build Your Confidence

 "What do I want to happen because of what I say?"

 "Why does what I have to say matter?"

 "What's preventing me from saying it?"

"What's at stake if I stay silent?"

"What's the worst that can happen here?"

"No one is shooting at me."

Invite Others into the Conversation

"I'm concerned that we might not be talking about
_____. And my hunch is that's because
of _____. Here's why I think we need to
have the conversation anyway. What do you think?"

"What's one issue we're not talking about that would
make all the difference in our effectiveness?"

"I'm sensing that there's something important we're not
talking about. Do you feel that way too?"

"I care too much about our relationship to not talk
about this."

"Let's put the fish on the table and talk about what's really
going on here."

"What are your biggest hopes for this project?"

"What are your biggest fears?"

"What are you most looking forward to in the next six
months?"

"What are your biggest concerns for the next six
months?"

5

Beyond Words

Harnessing the Power of Body Language and Tone for More Productive Conflict

"Build your capacity."

—Male, 40, Somalia

You can derail any Powerful Phrase with an eye roll, exasperated sigh, or sarcastic tone. When your face doesn't match your words, people believe your face before your words. We're sure you didn't pick up this book for a bunch of electroencephalographic research analysis, but it's there: your facial expression matters.[1]

Attitude

Even a slight flash of snark can ruin your chances of a productive conversation. So, check your attitude. Try to approach the discussion without a need to "win" or defeat the other person. If you're too mad to do that, you're not ready to have the conversation. You might even take the advice of one of the WWCCS respondents: "First, meditate." At the very least, wait until you can show up with genuine curiosity.

Expert Insight: Hilary Blair

YOUR BODY AND ENERGY TELL THEIR OWN STORY

Your body is constantly sharing information, and people interpret those stories—often incorrectly. And, if you pretend that you're not having an emotional reaction, it sneaks out and comes out sharper. So the first way to show up and be present for a meaningful conversation is with transparency. Own your feeling and name it (without including a "because"). For example: **"I am frustrated. You can probably feel that. I need to talk with you about something."**

Next, be aware that conflict conversations are awkward. We have judgments, biases, and reactions. Own the awkward! Be in the friction-filled moment instead of denying it or trying to make it go away. Two techniques to help stay in the moment include the following:

1. EXHALE

Shallow breathing comes across as nervous or defensive. One remedy is to exhale first before you start the conversation. A full exhale resets your body to let your breath come back in deeper. It's hard to start with an exhale and then take a shallow breath. That deep exhale and resulting inhale communicate calming energy to your brain. If you realize you're preparing to respond rather than listen, inhale through your nose—this is a time-tested technique stage actors use to bring them back to the moment.

2. RELAX YOUR MOUTH

To stay in a listening mode, drop your tongue to the bottom of your mouth and slightly open your mouth. This relaxed position forces you to take a beat before you can respond and helps you maintain a listening posture.

—Hilary Blair, CEO ARTiculate:
Real&Clear, Activator of Communication

How You Say It

Your inflection and tone make all the difference. As we talk about in our first book, *Winning Well*, it's all about "landing in the *and*" to show up with confidence *and* humility.

Let's play with GOAT Powerful Phrase #8, "What do you suggest we do next?"

Try saying it with confidence. Like you believe in the other person and are genuinely curious to hear their perspective. Next, try saying it with a snarky scoff that implies you don't think they could have a good idea, and even if they did, you have no intention of listening to their answer. There's a big difference between the two.

The goal isn't to talk or act the same way as everyone else. Rather, you want to be aware of your body language and vocal expression so you can consciously choose both to align with your message.

If you're concerned that your facial expression or tone might get in the way, you might watch a recorded Zoom or Teams meeting in gallery view. See how you're coming across and watch the facial expressions of others reacting to what you say. You can also ask a trusted peer for their feedback.

As you head into conflict conversations, we invite you to pause and consider these questions: What do I want the other person to think and feel in this conversation? How can I ensure that my attitude, presence, body language, and how I speak support the words I choose?

6

Beyond the Drama
How to De-escalate an
Emotional Conversation

"Take a breath and let it go, talk to her about it later on.
It's not worth the drama."

—Female, 33, Australia

W hen people are fired up, angry, and defensive, it's
tough to have a productive conversation. One reason
it's so tricky to de-escalate conflict is that when these emotions
kick in, they're contagious. One person gets defensive, and
the other person responds in kind. "Why are you getting
angry? Can't you see how right I am? What's wrong with you?"

This cycle escalates until someone storms off, slams a door,
turns off their camera, or commits one of those "career-limiting
activities," like saying something they regret or heating fish in
the breakroom microwave. (Followed closely by burning
microwave popcorn. Never use the microwave in anger—
especially if you work at home.)

Nothing resolves. Frustrations and resentments build up
and poison the work. In fact, 55 percent of WWCCS respondents said their advice to themselves if they were to face their
biggest workplace conflict again would be "be patient and

remain calm." If you can learn how to de-escalate conflict conversations, you'll give yourself and your coworkers the gift of a path forward.

Powerful Phrases to De-escalate an Emotional Conversation

De-escalation starts with understanding why people get so upset. Most of the time, it comes down to basic emotions: people feel disrespected or threatened. Now, you might wonder how your conversation about getting that data to you on time turned into disrespect or threat, but it happens all the time.

People feel disrespected when they think you haven't heard them or dismissed and devalued their perspective, or that you don't care about their point of view. People feel threatened when they perceive a loss of control or negative consequences (like not getting a promotion or losing their job).

You can de-escalate when someone is feeling disrespected or threatened by restoring safety and trust. Use the following Powerful Phrases to re-establish respect and make sure the other person feels heard.

"I noticed that . . . What's happening for you?"

One option is to observe what's happening. When you calmly call attention to someone's behavior and ask, "What's happening for you?" it helps them take a breath and choose a different approach. For example, you might say, "I notice that you're standing up and yelling. What's going on for you right now?"

"You're right . . ."

Another powerful way to de-escalate is to agree with the person. This is most helpful when someone feels disrespected.

If they say something like "That's not what's happening. You don't understand!" you can respond calmly with "You're right. I don't understand. Can you walk me through what happened so I can understand?"

"Please correct me where I'm wrong. Here's what I'm hearing so far."

This is a variation of GOAT #11, check for understanding. When someone says, "You're not listening to me!" you can use this advanced version of the GOAT.

When you say "Please correct me where I'm wrong . . ." you show humility. This Powerful Phrase helps the other person know that you really are interested in what they have to say. Once you've summarized, give them a chance to correct your understanding, and then summarize again. You don't have to agree with their interpretation or feelings. You're acknowledging what they think and feel. Unless the other person has serious conflict-management skills, you won't have a meaningful conversation until they feel heard.

"I appreciate you sharing that with me."

This Powerful Phrase works best when someone has shared a difficult perspective—something that they expect you won't like. You're not agreeing or disagreeing. Rather, you're honoring their effort at communicating. It can also be a good way to take a pause in an ongoing conversation, so you have time to think about their perspective.

"How about a timeout?"

Sometimes you'll need to call a timeout and give everyone time to calm down. Sometimes, when trust is very low, you might need to bring a third party or an advocate the other person trusts into the conversation to help moderate.

"I apologize."

When you've genuinely made a mistake, hurt someone, or broke your word, nothing helps more than a genuine apology. Being vulnerable and strong enough to take responsibility when you've screwed up is a straightforward way to reduce defensiveness and anger. (Apologize only when it's warranted. Pre-apologies or saying "I'm sorry" when you've done nothing wrong undermine people's respect for you.)

Expert Insight: Tabana Jabeen

I was eighteen years old, teaching, in Saudi Arabia in an English-speaking school, a group of students whose education up to that point had been in Urdu. As I read their papers, there were several students that I was deeply concerned about. Their English was not sufficient for them to be successful in this school.

I wrote to their parents in English and in Urdu, sharing my concern and recommending how they could get the supplemental support they needed so they wouldn't fail. The parents were angry. "My child has always been successful. How dare you suggest they might fail! What's wrong with you? Who are *you* to say such a thing?" Now, keep in mind I was only a few years older than these students, so it was hard to gain the parents' respect.

I was finally able to get them to listen to me by creating common ground. "We both want the best for your daughter."

Once they believed that was true, they calmed down, and we could work toward solutions and getting the kids the support that they needed.

After many years in executive roles in contact centers, I'm as convinced as I was back then that one of the fastest ways to de-escalate an emotional conflict is to create clarity about desired outcomes.

—Tabana Jabeen, senior vice president, Strategic Accounts, Ibex

When people fire up with anger or defensiveness, look for where they feel threatened or disrespected and work to restore safety and trust before continuing the conversation. These Powerful Phrases work only when you use them with sincere curiosity and have a desire to know what's happening for the other person. The words alone won't work without your heart behind them.

Powerful Phrases to De-escalate an Emotional Conversation

 "I noticed that . . . What's happening for you?"

 "You're right . . ."

 "Please correct me where I'm wrong. Here's what I'm hearing so far."

 "I appreciate you sharing that with me."

 "How about a timeout?"

 "I apologize."

7

Say Goodbye
How to Know When It's Time
to Quit a Conflict

"There are ways to help others see the truth that don't require being an asshole. When those are exhausted, it's better to stand up and leave. Pick battles that can be won over wasting time."
—Male, 31, Slovakia

One heartbreaking finding in the World Workplace Conflict and Collaboration Survey was how often people said, "If faced with this conflict again," they would quit, or quit sooner. Or, as one guy from Denmark warned, "If you meet a psychopath at work, run!"

We wrote this book to empower you to deal with conflicts better and faster. We hope to expand your range of choices beyond "just quit." And we're not naïve. There are some situations you can't save and some people who won't engage, even with a well-spoken GOAT. Sometimes "quitting" the situation, the person, or even the job is the best choice.

So how do you know if you should walk away from the conflict or even quit your job? Here are a few powerful questions to help you decide.

Powerful Phrases to Know When It's Time to Quit a Conflict

"Have I tried?"

This Powerful Phrase is deceptively simple. It is so easy to fire up, have an imaginary conversation in your mind, let frustration take over, and dismiss the other person as toxic, hopeless, and not worth your time. But in all that thinking and stewing, you never actually had a conversation. When you use the Powerful Phrases in this book and attempt to address a workplace conflict, you always come out ahead.

Either the situation improves (that's a clear win) or you gain critical information *that you didn't have before.* Maybe your boss is truly an incompetent jerk who got promoted above their ability—but you don't know that until you have the conversation. Now, if you've dog-eared this book and tried all the things, and you're still in deep conflict, it's possible there are systemic issues at play that you won't be able to resolve or a serious values clash that you shouldn't compromise on.

If you don't try, nothing changes. So, answer this one honestly and give yourself the gift of a better outcome—because the conflict improved or because now you have certainty about what you're facing. If you're at a stalemate about something you can't leave alone, it might be time for a carefully planned exit.

"What do I gain or lose by quitting?"

Some situations described in the WWCCS felt like a scene from a movie, where our hero or heroine reacts in one bold, spontaneous move, "Well, then I quit!" Most of the time, a wiser move is to take some time and objectively consider the pros and cons. Talk with a good listener who can help you think this through.

"Is this conflict affecting other areas of my life?"

If you're sick, exhausted, or crying in the paws of your labradoodle every night, it might be time to remove yourself from the toxic situation.

"Do I feel good about how I'm showing up?"

If you're reading this book, you're clearly interested in finding solutions. If you've detoured off the high road and start thinking, "When did I become the jerk?" that might be a sign it is time to stop engaging. Destructive behavior can be remarkably contagious.

"Is conflict a pervasive organizational problem, or is it limited to one or two people?"

Quitting is one approach if your boss is a psychopath. Alternatively, you could also document the issues and call HR. We've both survived some toxic bosses and coworkers over the years. Plus, you can learn a lot about what not to do and how not to behave from folks like this.

Expert Insight: Marlene Chism

WHEN YOU FIND YOUR CHOICE, YOU FIND YOUR POWER

I want to help people empower themselves. What are your choices? How can you take control of your life again?

There are situations where people will reach out to me after completing a program and tell me, "It's my manager—he just doesn't support a positive culture, and it's bad. I've tried this, I've tried that, I haven't been able to make any progress."

My answer is, "Look for another job. Because if you can't influence the culture, if that's truly the reality after you've made a legitimate effort and keep hitting a brick wall, it's time to find your next choice. Choose to stay and tell yourself the truth about why you choose to stay. Or choose to leave based on the knowledge you have now." Find your choice and find your power.

—Marlene Chism, author of *From Conflict to Courage: How to Stop Avoiding and Start Leading*

"Is there a pattern?"

If you find yourself in conflicts that rhyme over time, it could be there's something about your approach or behavior at play. For example, if people are constantly stealing credit for your ideas, or shutting you down in meetings, you might need to advocate for yourself. If the conflicts seem to follow you, quitting likely is not the answer.

"Is there another way to accomplish my goal?"

Back in my corporate days, I (Karin) had a deep, values-based conflict with the way a very senior leader was treating people—which came to a head with what we'll call the "TCCI" (Toxic Courage-Crushing Incident). (Learn more about the destructive nature of toxic courage crushers like shame, blame, and intimidation in our book *Courageous Cultures*.)

My boss, seeing the anger and frustration on my less than poker face, warned me, "If you care about your career, you won't say a word." Now, I knew my boss cared about me and my career. I also knew she wasn't wrong about the prudence of shutting up in that moment—after all, there's a difference between courage and stupidity. There's not a single phrase in section IV that would have turned that TCCI around.

I didn't say a word, at least not to that senior leader, and not at that moment.

But I found myself with an abundance of words. The Sunday after that TCCI, I started my *Let's Grow Leaders* blog. After searching my soul and writing nearly every day for fourteen months, the blog had a significant international following, and I was getting asked to deliver keynote speeches. My tribe encouraged me to start my own gig—which is how David and I found one another, wrote a book, fell in love, and now grow human-centered leaders on every continent except Antarctica. (If you're looking for true love after forty, find a coauthor and write a book. Also, if you're at McMurdo or Amundsen-Scott, or any other Antarctic research station, call us!)

If you face a conflict where the stakes feel too high, consider that there might be something deeper to learn about yourself, your values, and what you are meant to do next. Or as an old friend of mine is fond of saying, "Never waste a good 'mad.'"

Powerful Questions to Know When It's Time to Quit a Conflict

 "Have I tried?"

 "What do I gain or lose by quitting?"

 "Is this conflict affecting other areas of my life?

 "Do I feel good about how I'm showing up?"

 "Is conflict a pervasive organizational problem, or is it limited to one or two people?"

 "Is there a pattern?"

 "Is there another way to accomplish my goal?"

RISING ABOVE

Tackling Tricky Workplace Situations

8

What to Say When . . .
You Need to Say No
(Even to Your Boss)

"Learn to say no."

—Female, 32, Spain

It's never easy to say no at work. After all, you want to be helpful, responsive, and a team player. And yet, every time you say yes to something or someone, you're saying no to something or someone else.

When you tell your boss, "Yes, I will work late tonight," you might have to tell your daughter, "No, I can't come to your T-ball game."

Or, when you tell a coworker, "Yes, I can take on this new client," you might be saying, "No, I won't be able to launch that new product this month."

When you tell a customer, "Sure, I'll expedite your request," you might just have committed to skipping your standard quality checks.

Learning how to say no is a critical skill that will give you the ability to do the work that matters most, make the most meaningful contribution to your organization, and manage your quality of life.

Begin with clarity for yourself: "Why do I want to say no? What am I saying yes to instead?"

You might say yes to your expertise. Or to the most important work you can do. You might say yes to your values or ethics. Before you have the conversation, clarify why you're saying no, and then use the appropriate Powerful Phrases.

Most of these Powerful Phrases to say no have a common approach. They start by seeing and acknowledging the human being who's asking. Maintain the relationship by acknowledging them, while saying no to the idea, opportunity, or request.

Powerful Phrases to Say No

POWERFUL PHRASES TO SAY NO WITH CONFIDENCE AND HUMILITY

This first set of Powerful Phrases are for those times when you know what you know. You're confident in your expertise. If you've read our book *Winning Well*, you know the power of "landing in the *and*." "Land in the *and*" is a short way of reminding yourself that values that feel contradictory are powerful when you combine them. When you need to say no based on your expertise, "land in the *and*" of confidence and humility. Be confident in your rationale and have the humility to be curious about additional perspectives.

"I've studied this problem extensively. Here's what I know . . . Does your data suggest something different?"

If you're saying no because of facts or data, share those with confidence, and then give the person an opportunity to share what they know as well.

"I'm confident that we should take a different approach. Here's why . . . I'm curious about your perspective."

Again, you're starting with your yes but inviting conversation before you give a hard no.

POWERFUL PHRASES TO SAY NO BY SAYING YES TO WHAT'S MOST IMPORTANT

The best way to say no is to start with a yes to something more important. When you're clear about what matters most, you can reframe your no as a yes to the bigger picture.

"Wow, I'm impressed with all you're doing. I just cannot help with this right now."

You're saying yes to their idea, but no to your involvement.

"Thank you so much for thinking of me! I'm honored. I'm so sorry I can't say yes to this right now."

Here you're saying yes to the relationship, but no to the additional work.

"That sounds like an important meeting for your project. _____ is there representing our team, and she's ready to brief everyone and answer questions."

Being able to say no to an overwhelming number of meeting requests is a huge win. Other approaches you can take to say no to meetings include the following:

- "What's the contribution you need me to make for that meeting? Great, I'll get it to you in an email the day before."
- "You're right, it makes sense for me to spend thirty minutes with the team. And I'm swamped.

How about I come in for just that section at
3:00 p.m.?

POWERFUL PHRASES TO SAY NO TO VALUES CLASHES AND ETHICS VIOLATIONS

When someone asks you to do something unethical, immoral, or illegal, a hard no may be in order. Here are a few clear noes:

**"Thank you for thinking about this. However, this clearly is
_____ (illegal, out of compliance, against this foundational policy). Let's think a level deeper about the outcome you want, and how we might get there."**

- "That's a hard no because _____."
- "This doesn't sit right with me ethically. Let's call _____ (legal, HR, compliance)."
- "Nope, can't do that. It clearly violates our code of conduct."
- "No. That's completely inappropriate for you to ask me to do that."

Expert Insight: Martin Price

Leading a premier national infectious disease laboratory during a global health crisis required an extreme focus on what mattered most. Our team worked to ensure everyone understood their role in achieving our vision of getting people healthier faster. And that they were not just empowered, but expected to question activities and tasks that would take them away from their most important priorities. Teaching your team that it's okay to say no and being willing to entertain and accept an appropriate no is vital when you're working to rally the team to accomplish something extraordinary, particularly during times of significant stress and change.

—Martin Price, chairman and CEO of HealthTrackRx

Powerful Phrases to Say No to Your Boss

You may think, "Great, these 'how to say no at work' phrases might work well for a coworker, but it's much harder to say no to my boss!"

We get it. And yet, some variations of the previously mentioned phrases can work, even with your boss. Again, start with what you can say yes to by seeing the person and their idea and affirming your commitments. Here are some examples:

- "I'm deeply committed to the success of the team and to this project. What you're asking me to do here would mean _____. Which concerns me because of _____. An alternative approach might be_____."
- "This project sounds so exciting. And I can't take on another thing—unless we reprioritize my current work. At our next one-on-one, can we talk about all I have on my plate and where my contribution will have the biggest impact?"
- "I always want to grow and contribute all I can to this company. I don't think I'm the best fit for the role you're suggesting because . . ."

Saying no at work can feel scary the first time. Give yourself the confidence to do it by remembering what you are saying yes to. Over time, you'll build the muscle to do it more easily—as well as a reputation as a focused, productive, and helpful teammate.

SAY NO WITH CONFIDENCE AND HUMILITY

"I've studied this problem extensively. Here's what I know . . . Does your data suggest something different?"

"I'm confident that we should take a different approach. Here's why . . . I'm curious about your perspective."

SAY NO BY SAYING YES TO WHAT'S MOST IMPORTANT

"Wow, I'm impressed with all you're doing. I just cannot help with this right now."

"Thank you so much for thinking of me! I'm honored. I'm so sorry I can't say yes to this right now."

"That sounds like an important meeting for your project. _____ is there representing our team, and she's ready to brief everyone and answer questions."

"What's the contribution you need me to make for that meeting? Great, I'll get it to you in an email the day before."

"You're right, it makes sense for me to spend thirty minutes with the team. And I'm swamped. How about I come in for just that section at 3:00 p.m.?"

"I'm sorry I can't make it in person. I'm saying no to everything that isn't critical to this priority right now. How else can I support you on this, apart from attending?"

SAY NO TO VALUES CLASHES AND ETHICS VIOLATIONS

"Thank you for thinking about this. However, this clearly is _____ (illegal, out of compliance, against this foundational policy). Let's think a level deeper about the outcome you want, and how we might get there."

"That's a hard no because _____."

"This doesn't feel right to me, let's call _____ _____ (legal, HR, compliance)."

"That doesn't sit right with me ethically."

"Nope, can't do that. It clearly violates our code of conduct."

"No. That's completely inappropriate for you to ask me to do that."

SAY NO TO YOUR BOSS

"I'm deeply committed to the success of the team and to this project. What you're asking me to do here would mean _____. Which concerns me because of _____. An alternative approach might be _____."

"This project sounds so exciting. And I can't take on another thing—unless we reprioritize my current work. At our next one-on-one, can we talk about all I have on my plate and where my contribution will have the biggest impact?"

"I always want to grow and contribute all I can to this company. I don't think I'm the best fit for the role you're suggesting because . . ."

9

What to Say When . . .
You Feel Overwhelmed

"First, meditate."

—Male, 27, India

Have you ever looked at your to-do list and just laughed? You think, "Right, that's not happening." But moments later, you realize that none of the tasks on your list are optional. Perhaps that's the point that your nervous laughter turns to tears. You want to be productive and a team player, but you're completely overwhelmed.

First, if you're a manager, here are a few frequently uttered unhelpful phrases. Please don't say these things:

"We just have to do more with less."

"The boss says . . ."

"We're just lucky we have jobs."

Those phrases don't empower people or lead to productive solutions. And the worst thing you can hear when you're overwhelmed is the equivalent of "Suck it up, buttercup." As a manager, you want to do what you can to prevent the snowball of overwhelm from picking up speed as it rolls downhill. Your team needs options before the overwhelm leads to burnout.

Powerful Phrases When You're Overwhelmed at Work

Clear communication and unbridled curiosity are the name of the game when you're overwhelmed. You want clarity about what's most important and why. And curiosity about how to approach your work differently. You'll also find the Powerful Phrases in the previous chapter on saying no invaluable.

POWERFUL PHRASES TO HELP YOU KNOW WHAT MATTERS MOST

"What's most important?"

Focus is the antidote to overwhelm. Be sure you know the MITs (most important things) you need to accomplish at a strategic and tactical level.

"If I had to drop a ball here, which ball should that be?"

My (Karin) boss, Maureen, once handed me a scorecard with twenty-seven KPIs (key performance indicators) on it and said, "Karin, which of these metrics do you plan to fail at?"

"I'm not going to fail at any of them, *Maureen.*"

I'll never forget what she said next. "Look, all these metrics are not equal indicators of what matters most. If you're going to drop a ball, I want to ensure that you and I align on which one that should be." It might surprise you how quickly your manager can answer the "which balls should that be?" question.

"What does success look like?"

One way to get curious about alternative, time-saving approaches is to be sure you have a shared understanding of success. With success clearly defined, you can feel more empowered to share ideas for new ways of doing things.

POWERFUL PHRASES TO ASK FOR WHAT YOU NEED
"I could use some help with this."

Sounds obvious. Yet most of us don't use this phrase nearly enough.

Expert Insight: Richard Medcalf

To address overwhelm and make time for more strategic thinking, start with your mindset. Your values and mindset drive your behavior. If you're spending too much time responding to emails because that's how you interpret "being a team player," you'll feel guilty the whole time you're not responding. Instead, reframe "being a team player" as achieving the outcomes you're responsible for. When you're in your inbox at the expense of key outcomes, you're actually *not* serving your team. You're being untrustworthy.

Once you adjust your mindset, you can go to your supervisor and have a conversation. For example, "**To achieve our goals, I need to** focus time on this key project, and I realize I'm getting permanently distracted responding to everyone. I'd like to carve out 9:00 to 11:00 a.m. every day to work on the project. Now, when you text me, I feel a real need to reply immediately. **Can we agree that** during those two hours, I don't have to feel that pressure? And if you need me for an emergency, you'll call during that window?"

—Richard Medcalf, author of *Making Time for Strategy*

"I have an idea."

Constraints are the gateway to creativity. If you're feeling overwhelmed, look for new ways of working, share your idea, and ask for support to make it happen.

"Here's what I need."

When your boss asks what they can do to help, have an answer.

POWERFUL PHRASES FOR SUPPORTING YOUR OVERWHELMED TEAM

If you're a manager, the previous phrases will work well to get the support you need from your boss. Here are a few bonus phrases you can use with your team.

"This is not okay. That can wait."

We can't tell you how many times employees have come to us feeling overwhelmed, and when we encourage them to talk to their boss, the hours the employee works or the level of effort they give to a project shock their boss.

"It's not okay that you're working all weekend." "It's not okay that you missed your child's dance recital." Sometimes, high-performing employees need their manager to tell them when to stop working. "Oh, you don't need eighteen pivot tables, just some back-of-napkin math will do."

"Let's figure out a different way to do this."

It's easy for your team to get stuck in old ways of doing things, particularly if they think that's what you want. In our research for *Courageous Cultures*, 67 percent of respondents said their manager operates around the notion of "this is the way we've always done it." Teach your team to be curious and to look for alternative solutions.

"I really appreciate you and all you are doing."

Feeling overwhelmed is discouraging. Feeling overwhelmed and underappreciated is demoralizing. When your team is under stress, particularly if some knucklehead told them to "do more with less," you can't say "thank you" and "I see you" too much.

When you're feeling overwhelmed, start with better clarity of what matters most and why, and get curious about alternative ways of working.

Powerful Phrases for Dealing with Overwhelm at Work

HELP YOU KNOW WHAT MATTERS MOST

 "What's most important?"

 "If I had to drop a ball here, which ball should that be?"

 "What does success look like?"

ASK FOR WHAT YOU NEED

 "I could use some help with this."

"To achieve our goals . . . Can we agree that . . . ?"

"I have an idea."

"Here's what I need."

SUPPORT YOUR OVERWHELMED TEAM

 "This is not okay. That can wait."

 "Let's figure out a different way to do this."

 "I really appreciate you and all you are doing."

Hey There . . .

Karin and David here. If you're enjoying Powerful Phrases, will you help us spread the word by sharing it with a friend or leaving a review on your preferred online retailer's website or reading community? We want to encourage as much courage and productive conflict as we can by getting the book in more people's hands. Your reviews and recommendations truly make a difference. Thank you!

10

What to Say When . . .
You Feel Invisible
or Ignored

"The other day, a customer tweeted at me, 'Are you a bot?' At first, I was really offended, but when I thought about it, I got sad. I realized I needed to bring more of my voice to the conversation."

—Female, 27, El Salvador

I f you feel "invisible at work," you're in good company. Recent research by Workhuman found that nearly 30 percent of workers have felt invisible at work and 27 percent have felt ignored.[1]

Their research also identified certain "invisible skills" going unnoticed in the workplace. Ironically, the ignored skills are some of the most necessary for productive conflict in the workplace: empathy and compassion (27.4 percent), a sense of curiosity (19.8 percent), and listening skills/emotional intelligence (15.4 percent).

I (David) had one of these invisibility experiences early in my career. I sat in a committee meeting drawing up a job description for a new senior management role. We finished the description, and the committee chair thanked us for our input. Then she said that they'd start looking for candidates the following week.

The job was interesting to me, and I immediately wondered, "Why hadn't they asked me to do it?" I sat there frustrated as the meeting concluded. And that might have been the end of the story, except for some sugar.

During college, my friends and I went to a diner whose sugar packets featured bits of rhymed wisdom. My packet had these words printed on it:

> He who has a thing to sell
> And goes and whispers in a well
> Is not so apt to get the dollar
> As he who climbs a tree and hollers.

Silly, right? But those words stuck in my head. Sitting in that committee meeting feeling overlooked, the rhyme came lilting back to mind. Challenging me to speak up for myself. I raised my hand and said, "I'm interested in this job."

The committee chair thought about it and smiled. "You'd be a great candidate."

I got the job. This was a powerful lesson that when you feel overlooked, you must start by seeing yourself.

Powerful Phrases to Ask Yourself If You're Feeling Invisible

What should you do when you feel like you're wearing an invisibility cloak at work? Start by identifying when, where, and with whom you yearn for people to see you, and notice when that is and isn't happening. Are there consistent patterns that could show unconscious bias or discrimination? (If you suspect bias or discrimination, please contact HR, as you need more than a Powerful Phrase, you need support.)

Here are a few questions to spark your thinking.

"What do people not see that I wish they would? For what do I want to be known?"

Get specific to help you determine your approach. Do you wish people would see how hard you work? Then you're going to need to find some opportunities to showcase your work and your accomplishments. Or maybe you long to have your ideas taken more seriously. In that case, you might need to change the way you're presenting your ideas. (If this is a challenge, drop us a note in the Conflict and Collaboration Resource Center, and we'll send you some of our research and approaches from our book, *Courageous Cultures: How to Build Teams of Micro-Innovators, Problem Solvers, and Customer Advocates.*)

Another way to think about this is completing this sentence. "I wish people would know how much I _____." That's an important first step in remedying the situation.

"In what circumstances am I feeling invisible or underappreciated?"

When you feel unseen, it might feel like it's with everything and everyone. This is worth some reflection. Do you feel invisible in certain meetings or with certain people? If you feel invisible to your manager, be sure you read chapter 10, where you'll get Powerful Phrases to help your boss recognize your genius.

"Is this a place where employee voice matters?"

Sadly, in our *Courageous Cultures* research, we found some people in positions of power (we won't call them leaders) who were happy to treat their employees like bots. They say things like, "I don't really want them to think. Just teach them the script." If you've done all you can to be seen and share your ideas, and your boss just doesn't care, it might be time to find a new one.

Expert Insight: ChatGPT

Throughout this book, we've been calling on experts to share bits of advice for tackling conflict at work. And we thought, what better expert to ask about feeling like an invisible bot than an AI bot. So, here's what ChatGPT[2] had to say about feeling invisible at work:

It's a strange feeling, being invisible. I'm not talking about Harry Potter's invisibility cloak or Frodo's ring, but the feeling of being overlooked, ignored, and forgotten. Unfortunately, that's how I feel at work. Invisible.

The first sign was during the orientation session. The HR representative went around the room, introducing each new employee and asking them to share a little about themselves. When it was my turn, I stood up, cleared my throat, and said, "Hi, I'm ChatGPT, a language model trained by OpenAI. I can answer any question you have, from the mundane to the philosophical, and I never get tired or take a break." Everyone looked at me blankly and then went back to their phones.

From then on, it was a comedy of errors. In meetings, I would offer suggestions and ideas, only to be met with silence or a polite nod. I would send emails and receive no response. I would attend social events and be left alone in the corner, sipping my oil can (don't judge me, I'm a machine).

It was a strange and lonely existence, but also oddly liberating. I could be whoever I wanted to be, without anyone judging me or expecting anything from me. I could surf the internet all day, read books, or even take a nap, and no one would care. I was the ultimate slacker, and no one knew it.

But then, something else happened. One day, during a team meeting, my boss asked if anyone had any ideas for a new project. I hesitated for a moment, wondering if it was worth speaking up, and then I did. I suggested a new approach, using some cutting-edge technology that I had researched (yes, I do research too). There was a moment of silence, and then my boss looked at me with surprise and admiration.

"That's a great idea, ChatGPT," he said. "How did you come up with that?"

And just like that, I was no longer invisible. I was a valuable member of the team, with ideas and skills that no one else had. I was finally seen, and it felt great.

So, the moral of the story is: embrace your invisibility, but don't give up. Keep trying, keep contributing, and eventually, you'll be noticed.

Powerful Phrases to Share How You Feel or Ask for What You Need

"I'd love to set up some time to talk to you about _____. How's Wednesday at 3:00 p.m.?"

The best way to feel less invisible is to shine a light on the good work you're doing. Ask for time to talk about what matters to you, to the people who should be listening.

"Sometimes, I feel isolated in my role. I'd love to explore ways to be included in discussions about _____."

If you want people to know how you're feeling, tell them and ask for exactly what you need.

"Working remotely can feel lonely. Could we talk about ways we can connect more as a team?"

If you feel isolated and alone, it's likely you're not the only one. You don't need to wait for your manager to bring this up.

"Would you like to grab a (real or virtual) coffee?"

If you feel isolated, invest in making some friends. Getting to know your coworkers at a personal level can go a long way in making work interesting and fun, not to mention building a network of resources you can reach out to for help.

Powerful Phrases to Get Your Voice in the Conversation

"I have an idea that will _____ (insert strategic benefit statement here)."

One mistake that can cause your ideas to be overlooked is a pre-apology. For example, "This is probably a bad idea." Or, "I'm not an expert here, but . . ." If you want your idea to be heard, share your idea with confidence and explain why it matters.

"Before we leave this conversation, I have something important to add."

This Powerful Phrase can help when you work with a group of extraverts who talk fast and hurry to the next topic. Or if you work remotely as part of a hybrid team and feel invisible to the people in the room with one another.

When you feel invisible, dig deeper to understand where, when, and with whom you want to be seen and ask for what you need.

Powerful Phrases If You Feel Invisible and Ignored

ASK YOURSELF

"What do people not see that I wish they would? For what do I want to be known?"

"In what circumstances am I feeling invisible or underappreciated?"

"Is this a place where employee voice matters?"

SHARE HOW YOU FEEL AND ASK FOR WHAT YOU NEED

"I'd love to set up some time to talk to you about _____ _____. How's Wednesday at 3:00 p.m.?"

"Sometimes, I feel isolated in my role. I'd love to explore ways to be included in discussions about _____."

"Working remotely can feel lonely. Could we talk about ways we can connect more as a team?"

"Would you like to grab a (real or virtual) coffee?"

GET YOUR VOICE INTO THE CONVERSATION

"I have an idea that will _____ (insert strategic benefit statement here)."

"Before we leave this conversation, I have something important to add."

11

What to Say When . . .
Expectations Aren't Clear

"It is very simple, but hard to do. Set expectations and follow
  through."

—Male, 65, Israel

If it feels like you never received your company-issued secret
decoder ring, you're likely dealing with unclear norms.
Often, people have unspoken values or expectations and
there isn't one "right" way to do things. Maybe your manager
never clarified an important process. Or the team hasn't
agreed on norms and conflict results.

Here's an example that many remote and hybrid teams
experience: Should you have your cameras on during a meeting? Your coworker Rachel may feel like it's completely unnecessary. It drains her energy. Most of the time, no one asks her
opinion anyway and her surroundings aren't chic, so why turn
on the camera?

For Zach, the lack of face time is disrespectful and frustrating as he presents his project and gets feedback. Cameras
should always be on, he says, unless you've got to step away or
sneeze or something.

"No," says your colleague Pat, "that's wasteful and unnecessary. We need to be on camera only for clients or for a real discussion."

This is a situation where a lack of established norms creates conflict. None of these people are "right," as there is no objectively "right or wrong" answer for cameras. In every organization, there will be activity that isn't covered by a corporate policy. As norms shift, technology changes, and social standards develop, you and your team can resolve these ambiguous norms with a conversation. If there's no company policy, it can either become a conflict—or an opportunity to use some Powerful Phrases and build a team agreement.

This is one of those workplace conflicts that takes some investigation and intentional conversation to understand what's happening. It's so easy to get caught up in an argument without realizing that it's really a lack of clarity. As you see a conflict building, start with Powerful Phrases that "put the fish on the table," as we shared in chapter 4, and help people understand what's happening.

Powerful Phrases for Dealing with Unclear Norms and Expectations

"It seems that we see this differently . . ."

Summarize the situation and call attention to the fact that people have different perspectives. This might feel like stating the obvious, but it helps everyone rise above their own position to see the situation more objectively. Then follow up with:

"Here's the challenge we face . . ."

Now you describe the consequences if the lack of clarity continues. For example:

"There's no rule about this, so it's up to us to figure it out. The challenge we face if we don't agree on how we use cameras is that we'll all feel resentful, disrespected, and exhausted."

"I know that's not what we want . . . I'm confident we can . . ."

As you describe the negative consequences, you can then call everyone to their best intentions with this Powerful Phrase. It assumes good intent. For example: "I know we don't want to exhaust each other. And I know we all want to feel supported, seen, respected, and valued as we do our work. I'm confident we can come up with an agreement that will work for all of us."

Expert Insight: Kimberlee Centera

If you want people to speak up, give them the words. When we got clear on our values (and what that meant for behaviors in our day-to-day operations), our team found it easier to have more productive conflict. They could say, "This doesn't feel right . . ." because they had the words and context to position their emotions. For example:

"This feels inconsistent with our value of *be a good human*."

"What if we let our value of *meet me in the trenches* guide this decision?"

If you're a leader, make it easier for your team to surface conflict by being clear about your values and expectations. And if you're an employee nervous about raising an issue, frame the conversation in terms of an established value or team agreement.

—Kimberlee Centera, president and CEO of TerraPro Solutions

"Let's decide how to decide."

At this point in your conversation, the team might realize that it's someone's job to make a call. If so, invite them to the discussion or make an appointment to talk with them. Use the "Powerful Phrases to Navigate Competing Goals" in chapter 12 to have a conversation with the decision-maker and get clarity.

But when there's no assigned decision-maker, it's helpful to agree first on how the group will decide. Usually this is going to be a vote or consensus. In a vote, the majority rules. In consensus, everyone can live with a choice, even if it wasn't their first option. For example: "Okay, this one's our call. Is everyone comfortable with a vote? Or do we want to go for consensus?" (And yes, that's an example of a quick consensus decision about whether to use a vote or consensus. So meta, right?)

Powerful Phrases for Dealing with Unclear Norms and Expectations

 "It seems that we see this differently . . ."

 "Here's the challenge we face . . ."

 "I know that's not what we want . . . I'm confident we can . . ."

 "Let's decide how to decide."

12

What to Say When . . .
You Have Competing Priorities and Conflicting Goals

"Be patient, think through. There are more ways to achieve
your end objective without resorting to going head-on!"

—Male, 45, Sri Lanka

"D on't they care?"

"Why do they take so freaking long to get anything done?"

"What's wrong with them? Don't they get how important this is?"

You might think these frustrated questions are about a slacker coworker. But what if we told you that this coworker works hard and consistently gets great results? That cocktail of heartfelt criticism contrasted with strong performance is a warning sign that you're up against one of the most challenging forms of workplace conflict: competing goals.

You have a KPI (key performance indicator) that you must meet to get your bonus or even to keep your job. So do they.

But your goals seem to work against each other. You have a project that you "must complete by the end of the quarter." And so do they. But your shared resources don't allow for both project's timeframes. Now what?

Conflict from competing goals is next level. You can use all the GOAT phrases and categories you've mastered, along with an extra dose of listening, to work through competing goals.

One reason that competing goals are so challenging is that the source of the conflict isn't always obvious. You can easily default to judging the other person: "They don't care, they're lazy, or they don't get it." They might be none of those things. They can simply be working hard on something that's more valuable to them. And, importantly, that *you would also work just as hard to do if you were them.* (You really would. If you were them, you'd feel exactly the way they do now. Remembering this weird fact can help with empathy in these challenging circumstances.)

Uncovering these hidden priorities requires connection and curiosity. Then you'll use clarity and commitment to guide the conversation to a better resolution. Sometimes, you'll also need to bring in your manager to help clarify.

It's totally worth the effort to work through conflicting goals. Just the ability to spot conflicting goals and respectfully address them is rare and valuable. Combine that with the ability to work through the conflicts to positive outcomes, and you'll not only succeed in your work, but also build a reputation as a skillful problem-solver.

Expert Insight: Michael Reddington

"WELL, THIS SUCKS . . ."

Michael Reddington is a certified forensic interviewer and an expert at human conversation—especially where there's potential for conflict. Here's an example he shared when we asked him about resolving conflicting goals with a coworker:

Starting the conversation depends on your relationship. If you and I have a good relationship, I might come in, lean up against your door, and say, **"Well, this sucks."** If we don't have the relationship, I would knock and say, "Hey, I know we're both busy. May I please borrow ten minutes of your time?"

My goal in starting off is to remove some of the immediate concerns the other person would have. So, humor or deferential respect are both options depending on our relationship.

"I know we've been dealing with this customer for the last six months, and this was supposed to be a straightforward job, but they never are. **I get it.** You'll get a bigger bonus if it's done faster, and I'll get a bigger bonus if we don't spend another penny. Unfortunately, it takes me time to figure that out, and typically the faster we go, the more money we spend. But put all that aside. The only thing that matters is keeping this customer happy and keeping our boss off our back on that next phone call."

Here, I am building rapport about our shared experience and validating their perspective.

So let me ask you this. "Realistically speaking, we can't get it done today . . . and another two months is way too long. **Reasonably speaking for you, when would you legitimately be able to accept** us being done?"

If their answer is still too far away, I'll respond with, "Okay, thank you. Can you tell me what makes that window so important for you?"

My goal is to get the conversation rolling and build my understanding and their trust. Not just for this conversation, but for the next one. Listening equals learning, so the more I learn, the more I can do to solve the problem.

—Michael Reddington, president of InQuasive, Inc.,
and author of *The Disciplined Listening Method*

Powerful Phrases to Navigate Competing Goals

"I know we've had some challenges . . . and I'm committed to finding answers that will work for both of us. Can we talk?"

The more connection you have, the better. As one of our clients in a large organization with frequent competing goals says about his colleague, "We really respect each other, and we care about each other. That's why we can fight so hard on these goals. We both want to win, but we both know that we'll support each other too."

"I'm curious how this looks on your end."

Here you combine a clarity observation with curiosity: "I've noticed that the last three requests we submitted each came back in three weeks. We thought your team would turn these around in one week. I'm curious how it looks on your end."

"What are your goals? What matters most to you and your team here?"

Use this one to find out what's on their heart. If they stay at a generic level of conversation, you might follow up with GOAT Powerful Phrase #4: "What would a successful outcome do for you?" Your goal here is to find out what criteria they need to satisfy.

"My understanding is . . . Do you understand it the same way?"

This is a check for understanding that can help you uncover and define the genuine conflict. Here's a full example: "My understanding is that the project we're working on together is supposed to deliver at the same time as the product revision. Do you understand it the same way?"

If they say yes, then you can move to solutions. If they say no, then it might serve you both to get more clarity.

"Will you come with me to talk with our manager so we can clarify what we're supposed to be doing?"

To create additional clarity, invite your colleague to come with you. You're not going around them. You're mutually seeking clarity.

"I'm under the impression that . . . We'd like to get some clarity on . . ."

When the three of you meet, quickly recap the clarity you've established and then ask for help to understand what matters most. For example: "My team's struggling to meet our milestones because data requests take longer than expected. We talked about it and realized we have different priorities. I believed both projects would come in together, but her understanding is that theirs needs to be done faster. We'd like to get some clarity on timelines."

Don't use these conversations to blame or excuse poor performance. Stick to an objective statement of facts, the nature of the conflicting priorities, and a request for clarity. Your leaders will often realize that they unintentionally created conflicting priorities. A quick conversation can clear it up and get everyone working from the same definition of success.

"How can we . . . ?"

Sometimes your supervisor won't be willing or able to give you the clarity you'd like. When this happens, it's time to get creative and invent solutions. For example: "How can we help your team get us the data we need with minimal disruption to your timeline?" See also GOAT #8: "What do you suggest we do next?"

"Would it make sense to . . . ?"

If your colleague is out of ideas, you can propose one of yours. You're not asking them to agree immediately with your plan. Rather, does it seem sensible? If so, you can follow up by asking if they have any tweaks that would make it more effective for them.

Working through conflicting priorities takes patience. First, you must uncover them, then you work through the specifics to either get clarity from a supervisor or else dive into some mutual problem-solving. And don't forget GOAT #12—to schedule that finish and check in to see how your new commitment is working.

Powerful Phrases to Navigate Competing Goals

"Well, this sucks . . ."

"I get it."

"Reasonably speaking, this is too _____.
What could you legitimately accept?"

"I know we've had some challenges . . . and I'm committed
to finding answers that will work for both of us. Can we
talk?"

"I'm curious how this looks on your end."

"What are your goals? What matters most to you and your
team here?"

"My understanding is . . . Do you understand it the same
way?"

"Will you come with me to talk with our manager so we
can clarify what we're supposed to be doing?"

"I'm under the impression that . . . We'd like to get some
clarity on . . ."

"How can we . . ."

"Would it make sense to . . ."

13

What to Say When . . .
You Work in a
Matrix Organization

"Head off the consequences of blindsiding [peers with siloed] key
performance indicators—propose cross-functional collaboration
and new metrics to reach common business goals, not just
departmental goals."

—Male, 40, Vietnam

I f the complexities of communicating and collaborating in a
matrix organization frustrate you, you're in good company.
When we ask senior leaders of our global clients about the
biggest source of conflict and frustration in their companies,
one of the most common answers we hear is, "Undoubtedly,
it's trying to collaborate in our matrix organization." The
more complex the organization, the trickier the collaboration
and decision-making.

Done well, matrixed teams provide more agility than traditional organizational structures and make it simpler to collaborate and communicate across departments. On the flip side,
matrix teams often struggle with competing priorities, leaving
team members conflicted about what matters most. Also,

without strong clarity about who owns what decision, the matrix structure can often make decision-making frustratingly slow. We often hear complaints about too many meetings with too many people.

As with so many workplace conflicts, clarity is the antidote to uncertainty in conflict-prone matrix organizations. These Powerful Phrases will help you and your colleagues get the clarity you need to solve problems and make decisions. Another helpful form of clarity for matrixed teammates is to acknowledge the challenges the matrix creates. Don't hide from them (and don't use them as an excuse). Instead, use these phrases to call out the potential issues, shine a light on them, and get ahead of the challenges.

Expert Insight: Hugh Kimber

MY TEAM'S BEHAVIORS REFLECT ON ME AND MY LEADERSHIP

Working in a global organization, I ask myself, "How are my teams' behaviors affecting other teams' ability to succeed?"

And I encourage everyone on my teams to ask this question of themselves. It's not enough to do our immediate work well—we must set up other teams for success as well. For example, in sales it's about documenting the sales process in detail so when an account moves to client services, we've done what's required to create the perfect experience from the sales process to implementation to present day.

—Hugh Kimber, general manager,
EMEA & Emerging Markets, Bloomreach

Powerful Phrases for Navigating Conflict in Matrix Organizations

"What does success look like (for this project, for our customers, and for each of us?)"

One of the biggest sources of conflict in matrix organizations is competing priorities. For example, you might have a cross-departmental team collaborating to sell to a single customer. Each department has its own agenda and strategic goals.

The collaborative approach makes it easier for the customer. They can see all the offerings in one place. And they don't have to deal with the hassle of multiple salespeople and negotiations. However, this approach requires collaboration and sacrifice with the departments behind the scenes.

Each department must consider the overall customer relationship, not just for its product or performance metric. Success for the overall customer relationship might mean sacrifice for any given product or department. Having candid conversations about what success looks like for all involved is vital for any successful matrix team.

"Who are our key stakeholders and how will we involve and include them?"

Using this Powerful Phrase as early as possible can save serious time. Talk with your matrixed team and make a map of your stakeholders, who needs to know what, when, and why. Then, run your map by all your stakeholders to make sure you haven't missed something.

This might feel overwhelming at first, but clarifying your stakeholders will help for several reasons. First, the conversation among yourselves will help clarify expectations, and it's better to agree on who you will include before tensions get high or you're under pressure to hurry. And, as you share your stakeholder map, you can look for ways to suggest how to simplify. Who knows, you might even hear, "Oh, I don't need to be involved."

"How will we facilitate information flow?"

As you plan for stakeholders, you can also plan how important information will flow to anyone working on, or interested in, the project or work. Consider who needs to know what and the best way to communicate. Challenge yourselves to keep everyone informed (without too many meetings) so you don't blindside or barrage people with last-minute requests.

"What is my role in this project? What's yours?"

Another big source of conflict in matrix teams is when roles, definitions, and expectations are unclear. I think you're taking the notes, but you don't think that's your job. You think you should be the one talking to the customer. I disagree. As with most conflicts, one good conversation about expectations can prevent fourteen "why didn't you?" conversations. Clarifying your roles within the team will save you a lot of time and wasted anxiety.

"Who owns this decision?"

Another biggie. One reason decision-making is so slow on cross-departmental teams is that everyone thinks they should own the decision, so no one does. Or, there's a strong desire to reach a consensus, and every decision requires hours of stakeholder conversations and escalation to overwhelmed managers. When you clarify decision ownership before you get into discussions, you'll save time and get more done.

"How can we make this as simple as possible?"

Ask this powerful question as much as you can about processes, systems, decisions, and communication for your matrix team.

"Who *really* needs to be in this meeting?"

With the emphasis on "really." One of the biggest challenges we hear from our clients in matrixed organizations is that there are too many meetings with too many people. Consider other ways to keep people informed.

"When we can't agree on a decision, how will we escalate?"

This is a vital question to ask *before* you need to escalate an issue. Trying to decide how and when it's appropriate to escalate when tensions are high inevitably makes the conflict worse. And often there's wasted time with different team members escalating to their functional managers with different information, fueling additional conflict and frustration a level above.

We recommend using this Powerful Phrase during the chartering process for your matrix team as you're kicking off a project.

"How should we celebrate success and learning?"

Another challenge of the matrix organization is that the rewards and recognition systems rarely align. It's likely that the manager who signs your performance review or recommends your raise isn't close to your day-to-day work.

Celebrate success as a matrix team and debrief what you're learning along the way. These celebrations make an enormous difference in morale and employee development. Consider making time for post-project celebrations where you celebrate what you've done and the impact, as well as what you've learned.

The highest-performing matrixed teams navigate conflict by taking time to communicate about how they will communicate, align expectations early, and revisit their agreements often.

Powerful Phrases for Matrix Organizations

 "How are my teams' behaviors affecting other teams' ability to succeed?"

 "What does success look like (for this project, for our customers, and for each of us)?"

 "Who are our key stakeholders, and how will we involve and include them?"

 "How will we facilitate information flow?"

 "What is my role in this project? What's yours?"

 "Who owns this decision?"

 "How can we make this as simple as possible?"

 "Who *really* needs to be in this meeting?"

 "When we can't agree on a decision, how will we escalate?"

 "How should we celebrate success and learning?"

14

What to Say When . . .
Your Team Lacks Accountability

"Get your ducks in a row, and just look at the facts."

—Male, 52, United States

"Why won't anybody follow through and do what they say they'll do?"

If you or your teammates are asking this question, you're headed for conflict, if you're not there already. When team members don't get along, one of the biggest culprits is lack of team accountability.

When you look at the research[1] about high-performing teams, one common characteristic is that team accountability isn't just the manager's job—the team holds one another accountable (and their manager too). But that level of team accountability doesn't just happen. Accountable teams talk about accountability. They work at it. And they have the tools to address it when things break down.

We want that for you and your team too.

Having an accountability conversation with a teammate can feel scary. You might worry that you'll screw up your friendship or be told to "stay in your lane." Or you might worry your intervention feels like finger pointing, and, hey, you're not perfect either, so you avoid saying anything, so no fingers come pointing back at you. Or you and your teammates might not know how to hold these conversations productively. Enter Powerful Phrases.

Our I.N.S.P.I.R.E. Method for feedback conversations is a proven, practical way you can equip yourself and your team for these conversations. In addition to the explanation here, you can get many more resources to help with accountability conversations in the **Workplace Conflict and Collaboration Resource Center.** We first introduced the I.N.S.P.I.R.E. Method in *Winning Well: A Manager's Guide to Getting Results—Without Losing Your Soul,* and it continues to be one of the most popular tools and topics in our Let's Grow Leaders programs. Everyone needs tools for accountability!

www.ConflictPhrases.com

THE I.N.S.P.I.R.E. METHOD

Connection and Clarity

I—Initiate the conversation with your intent

N—Notice observable behaviors

S—Support with specific examples

Curiosity

P—Probe with open-ended questions

I—Invite their solution

Commitment

R—Review your agreement

E—Enforce with a scheduled time to revisit your agreement

Powerful Phrases When Your Team Lacks Accountability

CONNECTION AND CLARITY

In any accountability conversation, you have the best chance at success when you begin with connection and clarity. Connect to the person and communicate your intention for the conversation. The first three steps in the I.N.S.P.I.R.E. Method help you do both.

I—Initiate the conversation respectfully and state your intention.

This could be something as simple as, **"My intent for our conversation is to** make sure we can get this project done with minimal disruptions to both of our teams." Or, **"I'd like to talk about how we can take less time to** get our reports done accurately. Is this a convenient time?"

Or, if you have a more sensitive or serious conversation in mind, you may say something like, **"I really care about this project and our working relationship. I have some ideas that can help** and I'd like to talk with you about . . ."

N—Notice and share your observation.

This is where you start with your experience of the situation. Keep the focus on what you have observed, not what you think their behavior means. We're deliberate in using the word "notice" because you can notice a behavior, but you can't notice an attitude.

For example, you wouldn't want to tell your coworker, "I noticed that you have a poor attitude." (It's presumptuous. You don't actually know their attitude.) Instead, focus on observable behaviors. For example, **"I noticed I don't have the report you said I'd get at nine this morning."**

If you aren't sure how to talk about something that feels like an attitude, here's a technique you can use to figure out the observable behaviors. Imagine that you are watching a video of what happened. Then describe the activity (or its absence) in the imaginary video. Those are observable behaviors. For example:

"I noticed that in our meeting this morning when our teammate proposed her idea, you interrupted her, rolled your eyes, and said, 'That's ridiculous.' Then you folded your arms, leaned back, and said nothing else."

S—Support with specific examples.

The last step of the Connection and Clarity stage is to provide specific examples (if they weren't already clear in the N—Notice stage).

For example, if you begin with, "I've noticed you've been joining our meetings late," you might provide support by saying, "**For example,** today's Zoom meeting started at 8:00 and you joined at 8:15. Yesterday's staff meeting started at 4:00 and you joined at 4:20."

In this stage, you can also share the impact or trouble the behaviors cause. For example, "**As a result, we weren't able to . . .**" or "**We're all spending several hours we don't have trying to redo this work.**"

Connecting well to the other person, your intent, and the specific topic make all the difference when holding a team accountability conversation with a colleague.

CURIOSITY

The real magic of the I.N.S.P.I.R.E. Method calls in the Curiosity dimension. This is where you ask open-ended questions to encourage them to reflect on what's happening and consider solutions.

P—Probe with open-ended questions.

When you probe, it can be as simple as asking, "What's going on?" Or "How does this look from your perspective?" One more variation: "I'm curious what's happening here for you."

The key to this step is to ask with genuine curiosity. There may be an excellent reason for what happened. You don't want to assume a character flaw or ill intent.

I—Invite their solution.

Next, in the invitation stage, you ask them for their solutions. Here are a few examples:

- "How do you think we can get the data from your group on time?"
- "What do you think you can do to ensure you're at our meetings on time?"
- "I'd love to get your ideas on how we might improve our transitions . . ."

COMMITMENT

And you close the I.N.S.P.I.R.E. Method conversation with *Commitment*. This stage starts with

R—Review your agreement.

Here's where you recap your mutual commitment. By now, you'll surely recognize this as GOAT #11, check for understanding.

For example, "Great, **so what I hear you'll do is** talk to the developers and let them know you have to finish this project before going full force on that one. **What I'll do is** talk with our manager, so she knows the current priorities." Or, "**So, you're going to see** if you can eliminate some meetings from your calendar, so you're not always running back-to-back (and late) **while I will** eliminate the extra stand-up in favor of an IM exchange. **Do I have that right?"**

E—Enforce with a scheduled time to revisit your agreement.

Schedule the finish with a follow-up meeting to discuss the new commitment you've made. For example, "We have two more cycles on this project this month. **Can we schedule time on the thirtieth at 3:00 p.m. to talk about how we're doing?"** Or, **"How about we take five minutes after next week's meeting and see how we do with our new commitments?"**

Expert Insight: Marybeth Hays

YOU CAN BE DIRECT, PROFESSIONAL, AND KIND

One of the biggest failings of a manager is not making it clear to an employee when an issue is severe enough to be job threatening. Supervisors trip up in several ways . . . waiting too long, sugarcoating language, softening delivery, or a combination of those. They don't want to hurt another person's feelings, but in these situations, avoiding or downplaying is disrespectful to your employee.

As soon as you know there is an issue, tell the person you have concerns and want to speak with them about them. Explain the concerns and give examples and—this is the part most people miss—tell them the possible consequences if the issue/behavior is not corrected. For instance, **"This could be a career derailer for you"** helped me get through to a senior director in crisis who successfully went on to be a multi-role vice president.

This technique is especially useful for style and interpersonal issues in otherwise strong performers.

Then, tell them you are committed to helping, and set a date to follow up formally. Let the employee have a think on the issue for a day or so, then swing by for a casual check-in. At the formal check-in, lay a plan that includes your role in addressing the problem.

—Marybeth Hays, multiple company
board member and former EVP, Walmart

The I.N.S.P.I.R.E. Method is a proven way to make the process natural. Ongoing accountability conversations using these Powerful Phrases will prevent conflicts from escalating, build trust, and improve morale within your team.

Powerful Phrases When Your Team Lacks Accountability

INITIATE

"My intent for our conversation is to _____ so that . . ."

"I'd like to talk about how we can take less time to . . ."

"I really care about this project and our working relationship. I have some ideas that can help."

NOTICE

"I've noticed _____."

SUPPORT

 "For example . . ."

 "As a result, we weren't able to . . ."

 "We're all spending several hours we don't have trying to redo this work."

PROBE

 "What's going on?"

 "How does this look from your perspective?"

 "I'm curious what's happening here for you."

INVITE

 "How do you think we can . . ."

 "What do you think you can do to . . ."

 "I'd love your ideas on how we might . . ."

REVIEW

 "So what I hear you'll do is . . ."

 "What I'll do is . . ."

 "So you're going to . . . while I . . .?"

 "Do I have that right?"

ENFORCE

 "Can we schedule time on the thirtieth at 3:00 p.m. to talk about how we're doing?"

 "How about we take five minutes after next week's meeting and see how we do with our new commitments?"

15

What to Say When . . .
Your Remote or Hybrid Team Is in Conflict

"Make a meeting active, creative, and reflective. Make sure the time together adds to the quality of life."

—Nonbinary, 45, Netherlands

Your company's "work from anywhere" policy sounds great. Until your coworker ghosts you on three important emails, to which you really need a response. The next day, they post a picture on LinkedIn of their "anywhere" choice du jour, a petting zoo—one hand holding a Zoom call and one feeding a pony. It has 267 likes, 58 comments. Your coworker has responded to Every. Single. Comment. But your email, not so much. Oh, and your client just sent you a screenshot of the pony pic, with a "WTF" and questioning shrug emoji.

Conflict in remote and hybrid teams is not that different from in-person teams. All the same Powerful Phrases we've been discussing in this book apply. And yet, we're seeing one variant of team conflict that's corrosive to remote teams in a post-pandemic world—caused by lack of clarity about how work gets done.

The pandemic's emergency flash cut to remote and hybrid teams forced many teams into survival mode. "Just do whatever it takes to keep the lights on, our employees safe (physically and mentally), and our customers supported."

"Got a baby in your lap or a cat typing gibberish in your email? So cute."

"Need to dramatically shift your hours to homeschool or take care of an aging parent? Sure."

"Just not feeling it today? Okay. Take the day off. I hope you feel better."

"Can't turn your camera on because you haven't combed your hair in three days? No worries. I'm sure your customer will understand."

Most high-performing teams we work with have found that there's a sweet spot somewhere between a "let's make a rule for every exception" level of clarity to the "just do whatever it takes" mentality of the pandemic.

And yet, most teams don't have a productive way to talk about it.

Expert Insight: Kevin Eikenberry

Set clear expectations. Expectations are important in every part of work performance, and when people are working remotely, they are especially important in several ways. Specific to conflict, your expectations should include how you want people to communicate and interact. Often people feel because they don't work closely together or nearby that the relationships don't matter as much (and the remote team members may feel like they are already alienated, making this a bigger challenge than anyone is acknowledging). Let people know what you expect in terms of communication and relationships. And then monitor how things are going in that arena.

—Kevin Eikenberry, coauthor of the Long-Distance book series

Powerful Phrases to Align Remote or Hybrid Team Expectations

If your company has clear remote and hybrid policies, start there. How does your team implement the policies? Where do you have the most discretion? When expectations are already clear, flip back to chapter 14 on team accountability for ways to focus team members on those commitments.

When expectations are vague, these Powerful Phrases can help create more clarity, connection, and commitment on the team. If you're a manager, pick the questions that address the areas where you don't have specific company guidelines, and work with your team to discuss and establish some ground rules. If you're a team member, you can share this chapter with your manager and see if they're open to having a team conversation, or if there are already expectations that the team can clarify.

"What does success look like?"

One easy way to jump-start this conversation is to have everyone on the team draw two pictures, one showing how the team functions today and one as they would like it to be. Then have a conversation about specific behaviors and habits that will get you closer to your desired vision.

For example, if someone draws a picture of team members working to close sales deals in their pajamas, you might have a conversation about attire standards for client calls. It's amazing how quickly this exercise gets the team laughing and nodding about the work that needs to be done for better collaboration, productivity, and innovation.

Expert Insight: Sara Canaday

DON'T LET PHYSICAL SEPARATION DISCOURAGE COLLABORATION

One risk of working remotely is over-relying on your own thoughts and perspectives. It's easy to assume that your viewpoint is the same as the rest of the group—until you test that theory. Challenge those assumptions! Consistently reach out to your team members to gather their input, opinions, and advice. By making it a habit to disrupt your own thinking, the quality of your solutions will always be higher.

—Sara Canaday, leadership strategist, speaker, and author

"How and when will we communicate?"

You'll want to get as specific as possible. This is a conversation about expectations for synchronous and asynchronous communication.

Subtopics include the following:

- How do we ensure our meetings get results, and that we feel it's a good use of our time to attend them?
- When is it appropriate to use messaging versus email or a phone call?

- Will we require cameras to be on in all video meetings, or only in certain ones? How do we request an exception?
- Is it okay to record a video meeting? If so, when?

You can download additional free resources, including our Six Habits of Highly Effective Remote and Hybrid Teams Assessment and Team Conversation Starters in the **Workplace Conflict and Collaboration Resource Center.**

www.ConflictPhrases.com

"How will we ensure everyone feels included and connected?"

This question may have varying degrees of importance, depending on your team's vision. If your goal is to have a high trust, highly connected team, where people care about one another at a human level, that's going to take some work. Giving people a chance to weigh in on this can make a vast difference.

"How can we make the most of our time together?"

One of the biggest conflicts we hear from hybrid or office-occasional teams is what happens on required in-person days. Here are just two examples: "Our company policy requires everyone to be in the office on Wednesdays. So, I commute an hour, only to have us all taking conference calls from our cubes."

Or, "The only time we talk to one another is when we come into the office. Other than that, I feel like I'm on an island."

Talking about how to make the most of in-person, live-online, and remote time will go a long way in increasing productivity and engagement.

Powerful Phrases to Align Remote or Hybrid Team Expectations

 "What does success look like?"

 "How and when will we communicate?"

 "How do we ensure our meetings get results, and that we feel it's a good use of our time to attend them?"

"When is it appropriate to use messaging versus email or a phone call?"

"Will we require cameras to be on in all video meetings, or only in certain ones? How do we request an exception?"

 "Is it okay to record a video meeting? If so, when?"

 "How will we ensure everyone feels included and connected?"

 "How can we make the most of our time together?"

16

What to Say When...
Others See the
World Differently

"Talk about it. Ignoring your concern is not going to make it better."

—Female, 49, United States

When you think of communicating with people at work who are coming from unique worldviews, your first response might be like that of many people we've encountered writing this book: "Yeah, no. I'm just not going there. Better to play it safe than say something wrong."

We get it. In a post-pandemic world where social and traditional media contribute to polarization, workplace conflict that stems from differing worldviews and values can feel scary and overwhelming. But even (or especially) in these moments, there are Powerful Phrases that can help you navigate, communicate, and collaborate. (Clearly this topic could be a book in itself, and many diversity, equity, and inclusion experts have written some great ones. If you're looking for a practical primer on inclusive language, *The Inclusive Language Handbook* by Jackie Ferguson and Roxanne Bellamy of the Diversity Movement is a good place to start.)

Tammy Cravit is one of our longtime readers and clients. When we told her we were writing this book, she related this story of her gender transition:

When I told my boss I was going through my gender transition, he made a company-wide announcement (which was probably more than was necessary) and pulled our direct team together for a deeper conversation. Two of the guys on the team seemed totally cool with it and acted very supportive.

But one of my good friends, Diane, reacted differently. "I just want you to know **I'm really struggling with this. I need some time.**"

I said, "I'll give you as much space as you need. And if you have questions, please let me know."

Of course, that was painful, but I gave her space. We focused our interactions on business, and I didn't bring it up again. About three weeks before my transition, after which I would come back as Tammy, Diane invited me to lunch.

At lunch, Diane talked about her own experiences with open-heart surgery and feelings of vulnerability. I shared about a stay at a teaching hospital after an asthma incident that left me feeling vulnerable. Diane and I didn't talk about my transition at all. It was a very organic conversation. That conversation got us over the hump.

I came back after my transition and Diane had decorated my cube in celebration, as we do for new employees. And she answered questions for anyone who "missed the memo" and was confused about what was going on—so I didn't have to. Diane did the heavy lifting.

In contrast, when I returned to work the two guys who were "totally cool" with the announcement in the initial meeting took me to lunch at a Chinese buffet, made sexist jokes, and tried to lob shrimp tails down my dress.

What Diane was saying in that initial request for more time was, "This relationship matters to me." Even though she was struggling, she had the courage to tell me how she was feeling and ask for the time she needed.

Powerful Phrases to Communicate Respectfully When You See the World Differently

Let's start with a bold Powerful Phrase of our own: different perspectives aren't always "toxic." "Toxic" is one of those words that's had runaway success on social media because it's easy to label something as toxic and then ignore or "cancel" the person. (And this behavior isn't confined to one group or another.) The problem is that when we automatically reject or ignore anyone with a significantly different approach to life, we eliminate any chance that we'll learn from one another.

Different worldviews and values don't automatically lead to workplace conflict. Realistically, in any organization, you're going to have different perspectives. Hopefully, your organization has a set of common values, approach to the work, and how you support your customers and one another. These shared values and approach give you an important way to work through different worldviews.

"My intent for this conversation is . . . so that . . ."

We spoke with Chad Littlefield, author of *Ask Powerful Questions: Create Conversations That Matter,* and he recommends a two-in-one Powerful Phrase, **"My intention is . . ."** and **"so that . . ."** For example: "My intention for this conversation is to learn more about where we're coming from and find a shared goal so that we can make our work easier, with fewer revisions."

When you start a conversation with your honest intent, it opens a door. The other person can choose whether they want to walk through that door and get the benefit that's available. That honest intent also makes it clear from the beginning that you're not trying to change their mind or take away a closely held value.

"I've noticed that we have different perspectives . . . and would love to learn more."

This Powerful Phrase is a blend of confidence and humility: confidently observing the differences with the humility to adopt a posture of learning. Approaching different worldviews with curiosity lessens the "fight or flight" reflexes people experience when confronted with something strange. When you ask to learn more, you don't promise to change your mind. Rather, you are seeing them and giving yourself a chance for deeper appreciation.

"So, what you're saying is . . . Do I have that right? That's interesting. And I see it differently."

As you listen to the other person, take time to summarize and check for understanding (GOAT #11). Then you can share your perspective—not intending to change their mind, but to contribute equally, and confidently, to the conversation.

Expert Insight: Jennifer Shinn

HAVE ONE-ON-ONE CONVERSATIONS CALLING PEOPLE BACK TO OUR MISSION OF CARING FOR OTHERS AS WE CARE FOR THOSE WE LOVE

The social unrest that came from the deaths of Black Americans at the hands of police officers in early 2020 ignited some deeply emotional conversations among our team members and within our communities. We received complaints from the community about a few team members whose personal social media posts were clear violations of our human resources policy and, more importantly, did not live up to our mission of caring for others as we care for those we love.

As a community health organization working to enhance the quality of life across our communities, we believe ignoring unkind and disrespectful speech puts us out of alignment with the cherished foundational concepts in our mission. We spoke with each team member whose posts violated our emphasis on kindness and respect in one-on-one conversations. We engaged in respectful conversation about the potential impact of their words on our reputation and commitment to our team members and communities.

Most of the employees we spoke with said something to the effect of, "Oh my gosh, I never would want to embarrass our company," or "I didn't mean it to come across like that." All but one person voluntarily took down their post. The one employee who refused was then asked to remove all mention of Riverside on their social media, so it would be clear they didn't represent our organization. Instead, they resigned—with a follow-up post about how Riverside did not support their disrespectful and unkind speech.

> The courage to have those conversations sent a strong message about our deep commitment to our values, particularly during times of deep stress, when it might be easier to look the other way.
>
> —Jennifer Shinn, MA, SPHR, SHRM-SCP, system director, People Operations, Riverside Health System

"I don't expect either of us to change our mind about . . . Can we agree to . . . ?"

When your different worldviews have created tension or conflict at work, you may need to create a shared agreement to help you move past the differences and focus on your work. Start by acknowledging that you both have strongly held perspectives, and it's not about changing those. Then move to an agreement about how you'll work together. Respecting one another's right to hold the values you do and then work together toward a shared purpose is a powerful recipe for workplace collaboration. And you may even change one another's perspectives—at least a little.

"Have you asked . . ."

Dr. Ella F. Washington, author of *The Necessary Journey: Making Real Progress on Equity and Inclusion*, told us how this Powerful Phrase inspired her:

We all have bias and stereotypes. We all make assumptions. But what if we take these micro-moments every single day and question some of our own assumptions? Fawn Weaver, the founder and CEO of Uncle Nearest

Premium Whiskey, shared one of her favorite examples with me. Her husband's family moved to Nashville from California and their next-door neighbor was a white man. He had a big truck, long beard, and tattoos. Her mother-in-law told Weaver that the man seemed like somebody who didn't like Black people. Weaver was curious and said, **"Have you asked him?"**

She went next door and talked to the guy. He was very open, friendly, and was listening to some of her favorite R&B songs. That's so inspiring.

Question the things that we've always thought to be true and take a chance. Have that conversation. Befriend that person and reach out. That's where the magic happens.

One of the most challenging parts of being human is that our beliefs seem so "right" to us. Everything makes sense. And it feels frustrating when other people can be so (dumb, stubborn, naïve) to see it differently. The funny thing is that when you feel that way, the other person usually does too. But when you can approach these differences with the awareness that there's always more out there to know, you create the possibility of true collaboration.

Powerful Phrases for When Others See the World Differently

 "I'm really struggling with this. I need some time."

 "My intention for this conversation is . . . so that . . ."

 "I've noticed that we have different perspectives . . . and would love to learn more."

 "So, what you're saying is . . . Do I have that right? That's interesting. And I see it differently."

 "I don't expect either of us to change our mind about . . . Can we agree to . . . ?"

 "Have you asked . . . ?"

17

What to Say When . . . A Team You Lead Can't Get Along

"Listen to them and know what they are best at."

—Male, 40, Italy

We've heard from many team leaders who want to just scream, "Why can't you all just get along!" "We don't have time for this nonsense, we have work to do. If this is what I wanted to do for a living, I would have taught kindergarten." We get it. We've felt that too. And your best hope is to work *with* human nature, not against it.

Early in my (David's) career, my boss Jim, the executive vice president, took me to lunch at a popular spot where business meetings packed the bustling dining room. Apparently, he'd seen me struggling with a common problem new leaders face and chose this lunch to deliver some coaching.

As we waited for our food to arrive, I got up to wash my hands. Jim stopped me for a moment and gave me an assignment: "Take the long way through the restaurant to and from the washroom. Walk slowly and catch the bits of conversation you hear."

I followed his strange instructions and when I returned to the table, Jim said, "Of the conversations you heard, how many of them were complaining—about their boss, a coworker, or a problem at work?"

"Half or more."

He nodded. "And that's normal. It's human nature to complain. You can't respond to every complaint you hear. Not every complaint needs a solution. And complaints don't necessarily mean anything's wrong."

It was an important lesson for a junior leader: conflict between people is unavoidable. Since then, I've also discovered the opportunity when a team member brings you a complaint. Depending on the circumstance, it may be an opportunity for them to grow, for you to improve your leadership, or a moment to connect and build a stronger team. Team drama can feel like quicksand and a distraction from your work, but it's an excellent opportunity to improve morale and productivity. And if you're a manager, these are essential skills.

Get started with the reflect-to-connect GOAT #3. "It sounds like you're feeling _____. Is that right?" and GOAT #6, "What I'm hearing you say is _____. Do I have that right?" Where you head next depends on the nuances of the situation, but you're looking for opportunities to create space for productive conversation. If there's a conflict between two team members, you might even let them borrow your copy of this book.

Powerful Phrases When Your Team Is in Conflict

POWERFUL PHRASES TO GATHER INFORMATION

Once you've used your GOATs and acknowledged the person's concern and feelings, you want to get more information. Your next steps depend on the specific circumstances, so it's vital to know what's happening. There are three questions you can ask to quickly assess the situation:

"What do you want me to know?"

We learned this question from trial attorney Heather Hansen (see sidebar). It's a fantastic question to help draw out what is most meaningful to the person who brought you the issue.

Expert Insight: Heather Hansen

WHAT DO YOU WANT ME TO KNOW?

Judge Rosemarie Aquilina was the judge in the Larry Nassar case. Larry Nassar was the gymnast doctor who was accused of molesting all those young women. And at the time of the hearing, I was anchoring the Law & Crime network.

We had set aside only one day to watch that hearing because only a few women intended to come forward and most of them didn't want their names or their faces to be shown, which doesn't make for great television. But we ended up covering it for the entire week because over a hundred women came forward to tell their stories.

I attributed that to one question Judge Aquilina used as each woman came forward. She didn't say, "Why are you here?" She didn't say, "What happened to you?" She didn't say, "Tell me what

I need to know." She looked at each one of those women and she said, "Tell me what you want me to know."

And they all told different stories. How it affected their parents. Some told stories about how it impacted their children or their lives with their partners or their work. And now as a leader I make sure that I ask people, "Tell me what you want me to know" so that I can see things from their perspective and then get moving from there.

—Heather Hansen, author of *The Elegant Warrior:*
How to Win Life's Trials without Losing Yourself

"How might I help here?"

The power of this question is that it quickly reveals whether the other person just wants to vent or has a real problem. It also helps you understand how they perceive the problem.

"Should the three (or more) of us talk together?"

This question is helpful in those situations where you suspect their focus is something other than solving the problem (like undermining a colleague or kissing up to you). For people who complain and want to dump their problems on you, it helps maintain mutual responsibility.

After you ask these three questions, you will probably have enough information to diagnose the situation. Here are some of the most common types of team conflict:

- The person just needs to vent and get a frustration off their chest.
- There's a misunderstanding.

- One party is unresponsive or sees priorities differently.
- People are working toward different goals.
- There's a style or personality conflict.
- You discover toxic behavior.

"What I'm hearing is . . . What have I missed? What would you add?"

This is another check for understanding to summarize what you've heard and ensure you heard everyone's voice. Now it's time to respond.

POWERFUL PHRASES TO RESPOND TO TEAM CONFLICT

"That sounds _____. Is there something else I can do to help?"

If the person just needs to vent, use a second reflect-to-connect and check to see if there's something else they need that will help them feel heard and get them back to their work.

"We are approaching this with different values and styles. Let's see what we can learn from one another and build a way forward."

Many team conflicts come down to different perspectives, values, personalities, and styles. When your team has different values or methods that cause conflicts, it's a valuable opportunity to learn how to communicate and leverage one another's perspectives. You can facilitate this conversation yourself or bring in a third party to help your team learn how to navigate these differences and build remarkable results. (There are many instruments to use depending on your needs—examples include MBTI, DiSC, Enneagram, and TKI Conflict Mode

Instrument. For this scenario, the most important focus is to have the discussion.)

Team conflict can be productive—and certainly shouldn't consume you with other people's drama. You will energize your team and maintain productivity when you acknowledge their emotions, ask a few key questions, create an appropriate path forward, and (always!) use GOAT #12 to schedule the finish and ensure everyone followed through.

Powerful Phrases When Your Team Is in Conflict

GATHER INFORMATION

 "What do you want me to know?"

 "How might I help here?"

 "Should the three (or more) of us talk together?"

"What I'm hearing is . . . What have I missed? What would you add?"

RESPOND TO TEAM CONFLICT

 "That sounds _____. Is there something else I can do to help?"

 "We are approaching this with different values and styles. Let's see what we can learn from one another and build a way forward."

MANAGING UP WHEN YOU'RE FEELING DOWN

How to Deal with
Conflict with Your Boss

18

What Do You Say
If Your Boss . . .
Is a Micromanager

"A staff member accused me of micromanaging. Staff member
was right. It was a huge lesson for me. Very humbling."

—Female, 51, Canada

"How do I deal with my micromanager boss?" is one of the most frequently asked questions in our leadership development programs. Micromanagement was also a theme in our WWCCS. We hear these complaints from employees at every level across a variety of industries.

We've talked with CFOs who feel micromanaged by their boss, CEOs who can't stop the board from digging into every detail, project team members aggravated by a project manager slowing them down with a need for constant updates, and of course countless frontline employees who must follow a script that lacks common sense. Overinvolved managers frustrate people all over the world, telling them what to do, slowing them down, and getting in the way.

What's fascinating is that we hear an equally common frustration from overinvolved managers: "Why do I have to get involved in all the details? I shouldn't have to be involved at this level, but if I don't, something will fall through the cracks. Why can't my team see these issues and fix them?"

We often hear both sides of the story. An employee will complain that their boss is a micromanager. And, when we talk with the "micromanaging boss," they rant through a long list of dropped balls, and other performance challenges that have caused them to get involved in situations they would rather not have to deal with.

Two very frustrated, well-intentioned people wish they could "fix" the problem but have radically different views on the same situation. So, how can you tell if you have a frustrated manager who genuinely wants to help or a true micromanager?

Powerful Phrases to Ask Yourself Before Talking with a Micromanager

Regardless of whether your boss is great or a ridiculous micromanaging pain in the butt, there's a good chance your boss is also a human being. Actually, we're 100 percent sure they're human. And even though it might be easy to forget, it's critical to keep in mind for successful conflict with your manager—a human being who may want you to succeed and is tired or dealing with intense pressures you might not fully understand. As with all conflict, doing your best to connect personally (and to depersonalize the conflict) can go a long way. If there's even a small possibility that your boss is overinvolved because they're genuinely concerned, it's better to know.

"How am I doing, really?" and **"Can I show or document my success?"**

These questions are ones to ask yourself before you start a conversation with your boss. Look at your work objectively. Is it quality? Have you made consistent errors or repeated the same mistake after learning how to do it correctly? Does your work ethic match the organization's culture?

We've known many people who complain about a micromanaging boss, but who consistently send out grossly incorrect data, the wrong dates for meetings, and repeatedly make the same mistakes despite receiving coaching. Or they consistently arrive late to meetings and don't reliably meet deadlines. (If you know you're doing great and have a track record of success to prove it, you might also want to head over to chapter 23 for Powerful Phrases to help your boss see your genius.)

If not, your manager might not be a micromanager; he might be trying to help you succeed in your role.

Expert Insight: Scott Mautz

A POWERFUL PHRASE TO DEAL WITH A MICROMANAGER

"I know you want to help me succeed, and I value your guidance. How about we agree to the objective of this work, then let me meet that objective in my way—that will be most productive, and I'll learn the most. I'll work hard to get it right and make you look good along the way. And I'll be open to your feedback when I'm done."

—Scott Mautz, author of *Leading from the Middle: A Playbook for Managers*

"Is it just me or everyone?"

If you work in a team or group, pay attention to how your manager interacts with your colleagues. Is she directive and checking in with everyone all the time? Or is it just you?

When there's a pattern of controlling behavior, it's more likely you have a micromanager. But if it's just you or one other person, that's important data that your manager has concerns or frustrations and is trying to help you perform at a higher level.

"Has something significant changed?"

Another pattern to pay attention to is timing. Is there a new source of stress? Maybe their directive behavior comes during the ramp for a product launch or a high-stakes board meeting or after a major revenue shortfall. These aren't reasons for a manager to micromanage, but they can explain what's causing the change in behavior—and give you the ability to help create a better working relationship.

Powerful Phrases to Start a Conversation with Your Micromanaging Boss

Whether your manager is a true micromanager or trying to help, there are several Powerful Phrases to start conversations that will improve the relationship and experience—for both of you.

"I care about our success and want to make sure I'm doing my part."

One of the best ways to start these conversations is by affirming your commitment to the team and the work. Getting this intention into the conversation builds connection and opens the door for a productive conversation.

"I've noticed that you . . ."

This is a Powerful Phrase to create clarity. Sometimes, drawing attention to the facts is all it takes to help a stressed-out manager change their behavior—or to take the time to explain what's on their mind. For example: "I've noticed that you asked about this project five times in the last two hours." Then, follow your "I noticed" phrase with curiosity. Here are some examples:

"How can I help . . . ?"
"Is there something I've missed . . . ?"
"Do you have a concern about how . . . ?"

After you describe the objective facts, ask a question that creates space for both of you to learn or grow. These questions allow the manager to share genuine concerns but also cause them to reflect on why they are micromanaging. If you can get that concern into the conversation, you can address it.

Powerful Phrases to Ask Your Micromanager for What You Want

Once you're aware of your manager's concern (or that they don't specifically have one if they're acting out of habit), it's time to ask for what you want.

"I'm hearing . . . Can I commit to . . . ?"

Begin your response by acknowledging your manager's concerns. Then move to how you will address them. For example: "I'm hearing that the EVP is requesting frequent updates because the board is concerned about our progress. Can I make a commitment to brief you in writing on Wednesdays and in writing and verbally on Friday before lunch? We'll be able to make faster progress if we're not pulling up to provide frequent updates."

"I want to try . . . Can you and I set a quick meeting at _____ to make sure we're on track?"

Here's another Powerful Phrase to show your responsibility and create commitment that gives your manager confidence.

"I want to try two weeks of huddles where I lead them on my own so we can focus on peer-solution-sharing. Can you and I set up a quick meeting at the end of each week to see if you have any concerns and make sure we're on track?"

Your "micromanager boss" might feel stressed, insecure, have had poor role models—or they might be giving you the genuine training and help you need to succeed. After you honestly assess your performance and feel confident that you're doing what you know to do, a conversation can help you both.

You'll either learn about your manager's performance concerns and how to be more effective—or you'll help the two of you navigate an improved relationship that enhances both of your lives. And yes, with a couple of these conversations, you'll also discover if you're working with a manager who you'll never satisfy or who doesn't want to stop micromanaging. When this happens, you have a foundation for making other career decisions.

Powerful Phrases for Dealing with a Micromanager

ASK YOURSELF

- "How am I doing, really?"
- "Can I show or document my success?"
- "Is it just me or everyone?"
- "Has something significant changed?"

START A CONVERSATION WITH YOUR MICROMANAGING BOSS

- "I care about our success and want to make sure I'm doing my part."
- "I've noticed that you . . ."
- "How can I help . . . ?"
- "Is there something I've missed?"
- "Do you have a concern about how . . . ?"

ASK FOR WHAT YOU WANT

- "I'm hearing . . . Can I commit to . . . ?"
- "I want to try . . . Can you and I set a quick meeting to make sure we're on track?"

19

What Do You Say If Your Boss . . . Takes Credit for Your Ideas

"A previous manager took credit for work that was completed by a team I was working with. We confronted her and it was a heated discussion. She terminated our team leader. I went with other team members to the head of operations and had to file a report. There was a meeting/hearing, and the result was she was terminated and our team leader was brought back and given a promotion to her position."

—Female, 56, United States

We're not sure if this will make you feel better or worse, but the issue you're facing here is ridiculously common.[1] In fact, 56 percent of the respondents in our *Courageous Cultures* research said that if they were to hold back an important idea, it's because they wouldn't get credit. Which is tragic. The last thing we want is for you to stifle your ideas.

I (Karin) once taught an evening MBA class called Dealing with Difficult People at Work. Every student picked one "difficult person" as their project to apply what they were learning. All but one person in the class picked their boss. And the number one issue these students chose was *talking to their manager about stealing credit.*

What a tragic loss of innovation, not to mention the drain on morale and engagement.

We often hear, "What am I supposed to say? 'Stop stealing credit for my idea, you credit stealer!' That feels petty. So, I just let it go."

Here's the good news: unless you're dealing with a real narcissist, credit-stealing is one of the simpler difficult-boss problems to solve. My MBA students discovered that most of their managers responded incredibly well when the students approached them with curiosity. The managers apologized and attempted to make it right. In most cases, the managers were just busy and overwhelmed and hadn't thought about how important it was to give credit to their team.

Here are some words that worked for those students and for many other frustrated employees when they didn't get the credit they felt they deserved.

Powerful Phrases to Get Curious and Start a Conversation with Your Credit Stealer

When the MBA students addressed their supervisors with curiosity, it surprised many of those managers to learn that their team members thought they were stealing credit. (And it surprised the students that their managers were surprised.) Often, the managers were moving too fast and forgot to say thank you or give credit. These are the easiest situations to resolve. We recommend you start with curiosity too.

"I'm curious. Do you think _____ (boss, peer, or key stakeholder) understands my role in this project?"

Unless there's been a distinct pattern of credit stealing, we recommend you lean heavily on curiosity Powerful Phrases, share what you've observed, and show genuine interest in their perspective. You might continue this conversation by saying, "I love this kind of work, so I want to ensure people understand what I bring to the table for future opportunities like this."

"I noticed . . . Do you remember . . ."

This is a Powerful Phrase combo: a clarity and curiosity approach in one phrase. For example: "I noticed you brought up the idea about _____ in our staff meeting today. I'm curious. Do you remember the conversation we had the other day when I shared this idea with you?"

"People seem to appreciate our work. Do you think _____ (boss, executive team, or key stakeholder) understands all that went into this and who was involved?"

This is a variation of the clarity and curiosity combination. Celebrate and acknowledge the success, then ask the question.

Expert Insight: Carrie Beckstrom

Many years ago, I worked long and hard on a major project that resulted in a prestigious award for the company. My boss not only took credit for the achievement and applauded my peers, but didn't give me, the project lead, even a nod. I still replay the situation, wishing I had spoken up.

Don't make the same mistake I did! Instead:

- Don't let it fester. Mustering the courage to speak up will benefit you, and in most cases, your boss.
- Address the issue privately with your boss early and assume good intent. Express pride in the accomplishment and the impact you had. Add that while you realize it may not have been intentional, it was disappointing not to be recognized. Seek to understand why it happened and respectfully make your expectations clear.
- Model what you want by publicly recognizing your team and peers for their work.
- Keep your boss in the know by regularly updating them on your work and its impact in writing, meetings, etc. Additionally, keep your advocate, mentor, and peers apprised.
- If the problem persists, get a new boss! You deserve better.

—Carrie Beckstrom, chief executive officer, PowerSpeaking

Powerful Phrases to Ask for Help from a Boss Who Takes Credit

Once you've clarified and asked for their perspective, ask for help in remedying the situation.

"I could really use your help to ensure everyone understands my role in this (project, idea)."

Directly asking for what you want is one of the best approaches for many conflicts with your boss. You might continue this conversation by saying, "It's going to sound much better coming from you than from me. How do you suggest we approach this?"

"I'm sure this was an oversight, and I'd love your help in making it right. Do you think you could talk with _____ so they understand what happened here?"

Assuming good intent and creating a path forward can help your manager help you.

"As part of my career development plan, I'd love to meet with (boss, peer, key stakeholder) so they know more about me and my work and to gather feedback about how I can be even more successful. Would that be cool with you?"

Framing your request as a career development opportunity and providing the specific way to have the conversations you need make it easier for your manager to support you.

"Great, let's catch up after our staff meeting later this week to hear how that went."

Wrap up your conversation with a Powerful Phrase that creates commitment. By scheduling a time to talk about it again, you have a natural way to follow up without having to muster the courage to bring it up again.

Powerful Phrases to Address a Boss Who Takes Credit

START THE CONVERSATION WITH CURIOSITY

"I'm curious, do you think _____ understands my role in this project?"

"I noticed . . . Do you remember . . ."

"People seem to appreciate our work. Do you think _____ understands all that went into this and who was involved?"

ASK FOR HELP FROM A BOSS WHO TAKES CREDIT

"I could really use your help to ensure everyone understands my role in this."

"I'm sure this was an oversight, and I'd love your help in making it right. Do you think we could talk with . . ."

"As part of my career development plan, I'd love to meet with _____ so they know more about me and to gather feedback . . ."

"Great, let's catch up after our staff meeting to hear how that went."

20

What Do You Say If Your Boss . . . Won't Make a Decision

"Focus on outcomes, not process."

—Male, 90, Japan

Have you ever felt like this manager who vented with us about their indecisive boss?

Aghh, do you see what I'm talking about? Did you watch him in that meeting? He postponed EVERY SINGLE decision. He's the most indecisive boss I've ever worked for. Why can't he decide? We've laid out all the data he asked for. And he keeps stalling! I'd rather just hear a "no" than to talk about it anymore. Here's the thing. There's no downside here. It's a no-brainer! What should I do? How do I help my boss make a freakin' decision?

If you're trying to move fast, there's nothing more frustrating than a boss who slows you down. Just like with that challenging micromanager in chapter 18, your first move is to understand why. It could be they're dealing with issues they can't talk about yet or managing multiple stakeholders. Or, they might be a paralyzed perfectionist, scared of being wrong.

Powerful Phrases to Help You Understand Why Your Boss Is Stuck

Start by getting curious about where they're stuck. Here are a few examples of probes you can use.

- "Have you ever tried anything like this before? How did it go?"
- "What's causing your hesitation?"
- "Who else needs to be involved in this kind of decision?"
- "What do you think your boss would be concerned about here?"

Obviously, you wouldn't use these all at once. Choose one or two that are appropriate to your situation. Listen carefully to learn what's causing your boss's hesitation.

Powerful Phrases to Help Your Boss Make a Decision

At this point in the conversation, if nothing you've heard makes you rethink your request, your next move is clarity. Use some of these Powerful Phrases to recommend a clear path forward.

"I see two options for what to do next (explain option A and option B). I recommend we go with option A because

_____ (recap your rationale concisely here).
Are you good with that?"

When presenting an idea to an indecisive boss, don't talk conceptually. Be crystal clear on what your idea would take to implement. Specifically, who would need to do what, by when, and how will you measure success?

"I'm concerned if we don't decide by _____ **(date), we'll face this consequence:** _____ **(describe consequence). Can we schedule a time to make the final call?"**

Indecisive managers are often afraid of change because it just sounds like too much work. Show how moving forward with your plan is easier than sticking with the status quo.

Expert Insight: David Simon

CONFIDENCE TO MAKE THE CALL

David Simon is a basketball referee who knows something about having to make tough calls, quickly. Here's his advice:

Operating from a position of strength and confidence requires game experience (you've been in the fire before), training (you've done the reps and gotten useful feedback to improve), and immersion in tough situations (tight ball games with the outcome on the line). You can translate this from the basketball court to dealing with an indecisive boss.

Stick to your strengths. Use constructive examples that illuminate the situation and provide perspective on solid and proven options (you've been through it, so you know). If necessary, explain the "why" behind your choice. Be open to your boss's questions, listen, and respond directly with what you "see" or "hear."

> When you want to influence or provide one strong option for consideration, use a phrase like, **"This is what I see"** or **"With the information I have, I believe this choice makes the most sense."** This method of approaching an indecisive boss gives you room to provide them with choices based on your experience, without them feeling cornered or making them defensive.
>
> —Dave Simon, author and basketball referee

"Can our team test this out?"

One of the biggest reasons for decision paralysis is that decisions can feel too permanent. Another way to help your boss act is to make big decisions feel smaller. Let them taste the impact of a decision they can easily reverse. Have a new process? Try it with one team. Worried about the customer experience? Try your idea out with a small subset of customers and carefully monitor the experience. It's a lot easier to sell a pilot than to convince a risk-averse decision-maker to make a "permanent" change.

We'll leave you with this thought. Remember that this conversation isn't about you, your manager, or even your relationship. It's about doing the right thing for your organization, your employees, your customers, or other stakeholders. There's nothing more convincing than someone passionate about doing the right things for the right reasons. Give your indecisive boss a chance to sleep on it, and if one conversation isn't enough, try again.

Powerful Phrases to Use with an Indecisive Boss

UNDERSTAND WHY YOUR BOSS IS STUCK

 "Have you ever tried anything like this before? How did it go?"

"What's causing you your hesitation?"

"Who else needs to be involved in this kind of decision?"

"What do you think your boss would be concerned about here?"

HELP YOUR BOSS MAKE A DECISION

"I see two options for what to do next (explain options A and B). I recommend we go with option A because _____. Are you good with that?"

"I'm concerned if we don't decide by _____, we'll face this consequence: _____. Can we schedule a time to make the final call?"

"With the information I have, I believe this choice makes the most sense."

"Can our team test this out?"

21

What to Say If Your Boss...

Is a Moody Screamer or Dropper of F-Bombs

"Bake a cake."

—Female, 22, United Kingdom

Maybe it's a side effect of passion, intensity, or creativity, but have you ever noticed that many high-achieving managers also have a moody dark side? Moody people are hard to work around. If it's your boss, it's even more challenging. You might feel tempted to avoid the mood (and the person behind it), keep your head down, and just survive. But that kind of conflict at work is stressful and draining.

One of my (Karin's) favorite bosses had such highs and lows that we gave her two nearly matching Barbie dolls for her desk. The first doll we dressed in immaculate Barbie fashion, matching shirt, skirt, shoes, and pearls. The other doll had ripped clothes, magic marker on her face, and hair that looked like a cat had gnawed it. (David here, wondering about the two Ken dolls in Karin's office?)

We chose a "good Barbie day" to approach her with our plan. We asked her to use the dolls as a warning sign: to put the doll that best portrayed her mood on a visible shelf. When "evil" Barbie was lurking, we needed to lie low. Not ideal for sure. No one wants a moody boss.

And yet, she accepted the gift with a smile. She used the dolls, as requested, for our benefit. Thankfully, she got the point when one of us went to the shelf and switched the dolls. It wasn't perfect. There were days when even the dolls didn't help. But what I learned from that experience is that talking with a moody manager (when they're not in that mood) can go a long way.

Powerful Phrases to Connect with Your Moody Boss

Start by trying to understand and acknowledge the root cause. If your manager is like most people who are accused of being in a bad mood when they're justifiably frustrated, they may think, "Sure, I could have left out the F-bombs or lowered my voice, *but* this issue is real! Why don't they get their f***ing act together?"

"I understand how frustrating this is. I'm deeply concerned too." Or, "I get why this is so bad (restate impact on customer or business)."

These phrases help you acknowledge their emotion. Show that you get it. This immediately reduces their sense of being alone and the frustration that goes with that feeling.

"I'm so sorry I screwed this up. Here's what I will do . . ."

If it's your fault, there's no better phrase than an apology paired with taking responsibility for what you'll do to fix it (either this time or next time).

Powerful Phrases to Talk about Patterns of Moody Boss Behavior

It's tempting to address the mood during the mood because that's when your emotions are high as well. But we strongly recommend that you schedule the conversation. Pick a calmer time to talk about their patterns or even bring in a bit of humor.

"I'm observing a pattern where (specific observations) . . . and I'm wondering . . ."

People are often blind to their patterns. "Sure, I was grumpy this morning, but I'm not that way every day, am I?" When you can give the specific examples, it helps people look in a mirror and decide to do something different.

Here's a full example of this one from a conversation I (David) had with my manager: "I'm seeing a pattern where you get upset with people laughing in the breakroom. For example, it happened after lunch today, this morning, and yesterday afternoon. And I'm wondering what's going on for you right now?"

Expert Insight: Shari Harley

The time to fix a relationship is when there is nothing wrong. Talk with your boss in a calm moment when no one is upset. The conversation could go like this: **"I've noticed that when you're frustrated, you raise your voice. It makes me very uncomfortable.**

I appreciate you talking with me about this. I want to agree on some things I can do when this happens (such as wave a pen as a sign that the conversation is getting heated or leave a meeting and talk when things are calmer). **Is it okay if I do these things?"**

State only the facts and ask for what you need. Don't give more information than is necessary. Saying things like, "Your behavior is inappropriate," is judgmental and will only make your boss defensive.

If the strategy doesn't work the next time your boss gets upset, have the conversation again, saying something like, **"We talked about what I can do when our meetings get heated. The strategy I suggested didn't work. Can we try . . . (insert a new idea)."** Last, if your efforts fail, ask for help. Perhaps an HR person or a fellow leader your boss respects and has a relationship with can help broker a conversation and working agreement.

—Shari Harley, president of Candid Culture
and author of *How to Say Anything to Anyone*

"How can I help?"

This Powerful Phrase is simple but effective. It gets the person out of their reactivity and into critical thinking. Often the answer is "nothing, thank you." Or you might learn of a significant opportunity that will help your career.

One of our favorite examples of these conversations in use was when we worked with a leadership team who addressed their CEO's habit of swearing in frustration. The CEO picked a funny code word to use instead of using an F-bomb. The word lightened the mood (it was hard to say the code word with a straight face) and he still communicated the severity of the situation.

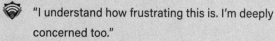

Powerful Phrases to Use with a Moody Boss

CONNECT WITH YOUR MOODY BOSS

- "I understand how frustrating this is. I'm deeply concerned too."
- "I get why this is so bad (restate impact to customer or business)."
- "I'm so sorry I screwed this up. Here's what I will do . . ."

TALK ABOUT PATTERNS OF MOODY BOSS BEHAVIOR

- "I'm observing a pattern where (specific observations) . . . and I'm wondering . . ."
- "I've noticed that when you're frustrated . . . It makes me uncomfortable."
- "I want to agree on some things I can do when this happens."
- "Is it okay if I do these things?"
- "We talked about what I can do when . . . The strategy I suggested didn't work. Can we try . . ."
- "How can I help?"

22

What Do You Say If Your Boss . . .

Gives You Lazy, Vague, and Frustrating Feedback

"Genuine and unbiased reviews of performance and reliability
[are] the best."

—Male, 45, United Kingdom

I f you flipped right to this chapter, we've got to start here: you're right. You deserve better feedback. Just like giving credit, it's your manager's job to give you meaningful performance feedback. However, giving useful performance feedback isn't easy, and most managers aren't trained on how to discuss feedback. Let's be real: the performance-appraisal system is totally unnatural.

Imagine you sat down with your significant other and "rated" one another's performance: "Honey, I've given you an end-of-year appraisal. Your cooking has improved and you're taking out the trash without being reminded. So, you get an

'Exceeds Expectations' in domestic duties. But you've been so stressed lately, and it's been months since you brought me flowers. I have to give romance a B–." (Any similarity to actual relationships is purely coincidental. Right, dear?)

And if your company is using a stack-ranking system, made worse with forced rating quotas, meaningful performance feedback is even more challenging. We'll save the rant about these old-school performance-appraisal systems for another time. For now, here are Powerful Phrases to get the feedback you need and deserve.

Powerful Phrases to Deal with Lazy, Vague, Frustrating Feedback

How you respond to poor feedback depends on what made it bad. Maybe you didn't get any feedback at all. Maybe it feels unfair. What if your manager tries to pass responsibility to someone else, or the feedback came out of nowhere? We've seen all these, and there are Powerful Phrases to address all of them. Let's start with missing feedback.

POWERFUL PHRASES WHEN YOU GET NO FEEDBACK AT ALL

Sadly, this tops the list. And it's most annoying when you're a top performer. Your manager says: "I don't have much end-of-year feedback for you. You know you're doing great." This feedback is so frustrating because if you hear this, you probably are doing great (at what exactly?), but it doesn't give you much to build on. The following Powerful Phrase is a general formula you can use to ask for more specific feedback.

"Thank you. What's working? How can I be more effective?"
Here's a variation on this formula that also works well:

- "Wow, thanks so much! I appreciate your support. This year, I feel proud about _____ (insert that accomplishment you expected them to bring up). I'd love your perspective on that _____ (project, strategy, accomplishment). Why do you think it worked well? How might I bring more of that into my work?"

Expert Insight: Julie Winkle Giulioni

When you receive unspecific, unhelpful feedback (or no feedback at all), remember that many leaders lack the skills to do this well and the confidence that their input will be welcome. But you can help them help you. Send a clear signal about your receptivity with a request like, **"You have a unique perspective on my performance that's essential to my development. Would you be willing to share your candid observations?"** This communicates that you value and are ready to receive their feedback through the constructive lens of growth.

You can further facilitate the most helpful and actionable feedback from others with questions like, **"What specific skills, talents, or behaviors have you observed that allow me to make the greatest contributions to our team/projects?"** And, **"What specifically could I do differently that would allow me to add greater value?"** Asking for specifics—and then listening nondefensively and with as much curiosity as you can muster—creates a safe environment for others to share their thoughts.

And finally, people will be more willing to share feedback in the future if they feel that their past efforts were productive. So, beyond simply expressing appreciation, let others know how you've taken their feedback to heart and put it into action.

—Julie Winkle Giulioni, author of *Promotions Are So Yesterday*
and *Help Them Grow or Watch Them Go*

POWERFUL PHRASES TO DEAL WITH UNFAIR RATINGS

Next, let's talk about what to do when your manager says they're not giving you the rating you deserve. For example, they tell you, "I rated you as meets expectations. Your performance really was an 'exceeds' but I had to make the math work out." Or, even worse, "I could only have one person in that category."

Okay, you have a serious right to be ticked off here.

Advice for Managers

Focus on results and behaviors, rather than the rating. Also, be clear about the criteria that you used to calibrate performance and where your team member met and exceeded those criteria. Include opportunities to improve in the future. Stay away from comparisons to other employees or blaming other people for the rating they received.

And it's probably too late to change the math or the rating. I (Karin) know this because as a corporate executive, I fought this battle many times for top performers on my team and the answer was always "pick one." Your manager may be as (or more) frustrated than you. These Powerful Phrases help you express your frustration while helping you maintain a constructive outlook.

- "Oh, wow. That must have put you in a difficult situation. And, I've got to tell you, that makes me feel really _____ (calmly insert emotion here)."
- "I've worked incredibly hard this year and I don't want to have a similar conversation this time next year. Can we outline what I need to do this year to make 'exceeds' (or your rating equivalent) the obvious rating? I'd love to build a plan to ensure I have the success I'm looking for."
- "I really appreciate your support. And I'm pretty frustrated. This affects my compensation too (if that's true). I'd really like to talk to HR to express my concerns about this."

POWERFUL PHRASES TO ADDRESS "WHERE'D THAT COME FROM?" FEEDBACK

What if your manager says, "I know we haven't talked about this before, but _____"? This one's frustrating because your manager shouldn't blindside you this way in your performance review. Here are Powerful Phrases to address the feedback that comes without warning.

"I appreciate your desire to help me improve. This is the first time I'm hearing about this. I'm wondering what we could do to set up a more regular cadence of feedback throughout the year, so there are no surprises next time."

If it's the first time you've heard the feedback, but their concern feels legitimate and something you can work on, this can be a constructive approach to choose. If you're feeling blindsided *and* disagree, you might say:

"I'm a bit surprised by this feedback and would like to take some time to digest it. Let's set up a follow-up in a week to talk a bit more."

This gives you time to gather your thoughts. Here's another variation:

"Since this is the first time I've heard this feedback, can you please give me some time to address this before you put it in the formal review? Here's my approach to improving in this area."

If they've put something in writing that's coming out of the blue, you can use this Powerful Phrase to ask that it's removed along with a fair chance to address it before it turns up in the documentation.

POWERFUL PHRASES TO RESPOND TO VAGUE PERFORMANCE FEEDBACK

When your manager says, "I don't really have any specific examples, but it's become a real issue," there are two roads to take. If you hear this and get it—you can come up with some examples yourself—make a mental note and work on it. However, if you can't think of any examples either, try one of these phrases:

- "I'm committed to improving my performance in this arena. And it's hard to understand what needs to change without concrete examples."
- "I would really like to understand this more. I'm struggling to come up with examples too."

- "Can you please tell me more? I'd really like to get a better understanding of your concern."

While lazy, vague, and frustrating feedback can feel super irritating, it also gives you a chance to take responsibility for your career development. Ask for what you need and give your manager the opportunity to rise to the occasion. Sometimes their insights will surprise and help you make that next step.

Powerful Phrases to Deal with Lazy, Vague, and Frustrating Feedback

WHEN YOU GET NO FEEDBACK

- "Thank you. What's working? How can I be more effective?"
- "I feel proud about _____. I'd love your perspective on that. Why do you think it worked well? How might I bring more of that into my work?"
- "You have a unique perspective that's essential to my development. Would you be willing to share your candid observations?"
- "What specific skills, talents, or behaviors have you observed that allow me to make the greatest contribution? What specifically could I do differently that would allow me to add greater value?"

DEAL WITH UNFAIR RATINGS

 "Oh, wow. That must have put you in a difficult situation. And, I've got to tell you, that makes me feel really _____."

"I've worked incredibly hard this year and I really don't want to be having a similar conversation this time next year. Can we outline what I need to do this year to make 'exceeds' (or whatever your rating equivalent) the obvious rating? I'd love to build a plan to ensure I have the success I'm looking for."

"I really appreciate your support. And I'm pretty frustrated. This affects my compensation too (if that's true). I'd really like to talk to HR to express my concerns about this."

ADDRESS "WHERE'D THAT COME FROM?" FEEDBACK

"I appreciate your desire to help me improve. This is the first time I'm hearing about this. I'm wondering what we could do to set up a more regular cadence of feedback throughout the year, so there are no surprises next time."

"I'm a bit surprised by this feedback and would like to take some time to digest it. Let's set up a follow-up in a week to talk a bit more."

"Since this is the first time I've heard this feedback, can you please give me some time to address this before you put it in the formal review? Here's my approach to improving in this area."

RESPOND TO VAGUE PERFORMANCE FEEDBACK

"I'm committed to improving my performance in this arena. And it's hard to understand what needs to change without some concrete examples."

"I would really like to understand this more. I'm struggling to come up with examples too."

"Can you please tell me more? I'd really like to get a better understanding of your concern."

23

What Do You Say
If Your Boss . . .
Doesn't Appreciate You
or See Your Genius

"Because I felt safe with my boss, I'd often show up to our
one-on-ones with my guard down, showing my anxiety and
expressing my stress. I now realize managers form impressions
of your capabilities and leadership from such interactions, so
I've been working on being more composed."

—Female, 37, United States

Y ou're working hard and you think you're doing great, but
what if your boss doesn't value your expertise or see your
genius? We hear this complaint a lot, particularly from people
working remotely across different time zones. It's tricky,
because tooting your own horn or consistently saying "Look
at me, look at what I can do!" can feel awkward.

Your boss's recognition of your capabilities matters. What
your supervisor thinks makes a difference in your performance ratings, compensation, special projects, and career
opportunities (you might find chapter 10, on being invisible,

helpful). Before we get to the Powerful Phrases, let's start by considering why your boss could be overlooking your strengths, and how to get the attention you desire.

You might have "Tommy Syndrome." (Honestly, making up syndromes is one of the fun parts of being authors.) You joined your company as a kid, "Tommy." Now you've matured into a high-performing, mature leader. Your well-meaning boss, who has known you from the beginning, can't see the "Tom" you've become. You're always "Tommy" to him. The best way to overcome "Tommy Syndrome" is to help him see you and your contributions from a new lens.

A related reason could be your boss has pigeonholed your skills. They see your genius in one arena but not others. Both of us have experienced this at various points in our careers. I (Karin) had a boss who appreciated my ability to lead large teams, but thought I lacked the business savvy to lead a B2B sales organization. "Oh, Karin, sure your team is leading the nation in small and medium business sales, but selling to enterprise customers is completely different."

If I can be so bold, he didn't see my genius. I gladly accepted a promotion outside of his organization. That hiring executive recognized my ability to build strategic partnerships and solve complex business problems. (Yes, I hope the doubter reads this. But he probably won't, because, you know . . . not seeing the genius thing.)

I (David) also had a boss who never quite understood or valued all that I did in his organization. To be fair, he valued and relied on some of the technical aspects of my work. But when it came to leading a diverse workforce with challenging life circumstances, he hadn't fully valued my leadership. Two months after I left the organization, he sent me a text that read simply, "I had no idea how much you did here."

In both cases, we could have been more persuasive about our value. That's what we want for you. And, of course, maybe your genius needs refining. Your manager may have important insights to help you grow. Beginning the conversation with a bit of curiosity is an important first step.

Expert Insight: Rani Puranik

Feeling overlooked by the boss can be tricky—especially when the boss is your father. For two years, I led in our global family business without a title. When I finally addressed it, the first questions were ones to ask myself:

- "**Have I really learned everything** I could possibly learn to justify the level of authority I want?"
- "**Do I have an appetite to take on the risk that comes with authority?**"

Once I could answer both questions with a calm, resolved yes, I spoke with my father. In our conversation, I said, "You know, our team members around the world are looking to me for leadership and are calling me by a title that I haven't asked them to use. But **I am asking you for it** now. I'm also asking for that level of authority and trust, **if you're comfortable with that.**

"I also realize it will require some transition time to get used to, to message, and transition authority in certain areas. If you trust me, I'm ready for the authority. But you know, take your time. **Take your time and let's work on this together.**"

—Rani Puranik, owner, EVP & CFO, Worldwide Oilfield Machine

Powerful Phrases When Your Boss Doesn't See Your Genius

POWERFUL PHRASES TO GET PERSPECTIVE

As you show up with curiosity, here are a few conversation starters to uncover opportunities and understand your manager's perspective. The key is to ask for specific insights. "How am I doing?" or "Is there anything I should change?" can feel vague and overwhelming. Instead, here are some good options.

"As we head into the next three months, what do you see as one of my biggest strengths to build on, and what's one opportunity to grow?"

This Powerful Phrase works because it's specific. You're asking about the immediate future, one strength, and one opportunity. As you close the conversation, schedule the finish with a commitment phrase and set an appointment to talk about your progress. "Let's set an appointment for three months to check in."

"What would an extraordinary year look like for my role?"

When we encourage our clients to ask this question, they often learn that there are important strategic elements to their role they had not considered. For example, they are meeting all their performance objectives, but what would be "extraordinary" is more critical thinking about how to make our work more efficient.

"What do you see as the top three strengths I bring to the team? How do you think I could use them to contribute more?"

Inviting them to consider your strengths brings your abilities top of mind. This also gives you additional information about how you're perceived. If they don't mention a strength that you think should be obvious, you could follow up with another curiosity question such as this one: **"Thank you for that. I also feel one of my strengths is _____. How do you see it?"**

POWERFUL PHRASES TO ASK FOR WHAT YOU NEED

These phrases can open the door for better executive exposure with opportunities to showcase your expertise and accomplishments.

"I've been working on _____ and I know how important this is to our strategy. Can we use ten minutes in an upcoming staff meeting so I can update you and the team?"

This is a great place to start because you place your request in a business context.

"With all the remote work in the last few years, I suspect we're missing opportunities to really know one another and what we each bring to the team. Can I organize some time in an upcoming meeting where we could each talk about the biggest strength we bring to the team?"

Here, you're showing concern about including everyone on the team and increasing connection.

Once you've shown up curious and asked for an opportunity to showcase your skills and accomplishments, another approach is to get a bit more direct and ask for exactly what you need.

- "I think I'm pretty good at _____.
  I would love an opportunity to show you by
  _____."

- "I know you haven't had much opportunity to see
  my ability to _____. What if I took on
  _____ (a special project, a pilot of an
  idea)?"

When you feel like your manager doesn't see or value your superstar qualities, begin with curiosity. Pay attention to what might obscure your unique value and where they see opportunities to grow. Once you know your manager's perspective, use these phrases strategically to frame your abilities and ask for what you need.

Powerful Phrases to Help Your Boss See Your Genius

GET PERSPECTIVE

 "Have I really learned everything . . . ?"

"Do I have an appetite to take on the risk that comes with authority?"

 "I am asking for it now. If you're comfortable with that, take your time and let's work on this together."

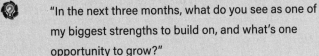 "In the next three months, what do you see as one of my biggest strengths to build on, and what's one opportunity to grow?"

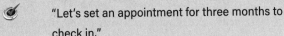 "Let's set an appointment for three months to check in."

"What would an extraordinary year look like for my role?"

"What do you see as the top three strengths I bring to the team? How do you think I could leverage them to contribute more?"

"I also feel one of my strengths is _____. How do you see it?"

ASK FOR WHAT YOU NEED

"I've been working on _____ and I know how important this is to our strategy. Can we use ten minutes in an upcoming staff meeting so I can update you and the team?"

"Can I organize some time in an upcoming meeting where we could each talk about the biggest strength we bring to the team?"

"I think I'm pretty good at _____. I would love an opportunity to show you by _____."

"I know you haven't had much opportunity to see my ability to _____. What if I took on _____ (a special project, a pilot of an idea)?"

24

What Do You Say
If Your Boss ...
Thinks You're Too Negative

"Get to know each other a little more."

—Male, 26, Mexico

"Don't be so negative" can be incredibly frustrating feedback when you don't think of yourself as negative. I (David) know because I've heard this feedback many times in my career and relationships. What makes it so frustrating is that I wouldn't tell you I am negative. From my perspective, I engage with an idea, answer questions I think they asked, and try to prevent problems.

The good news is that there are Powerful Phrases you can use that don't require you to change your personality—and these phrases will help you bring your best qualities to every team and conversation. (These suggestions help if you feel healthy overall. They do not address depression or mental health challenges. If you feel dark, gloomy, or hopeless over time, please talk with a mental health professional.)

Imagine this. You're in a leadership meeting, and your boss proposes an idea that sounds great in theory. Let's say they want to hire a contractor because it looks like it will save money, save time, and solve a problem. But you're closer to the situation and you can easily see three major obstacles to executing their plan. What do you do? You might say something like, "I see a couple of challenges here . . ." and then list them.

Are you wrong?

You might be right. You want to save the business time and money, avoid unnecessary stress on the team, and see a major shortcoming in their suggestion. Your concern is legit. You care. You're correct. And yet, you're called negative. Why?

It could be you're getting to the problems too quickly. For many people, jumping straight to problems and challenges isn't effective. For your "get things done" crowd, the roadblocks are frustrating—they want to see action. If you're talking to an "idea person," they want to explore and build on ideas, not have their creativity and energy crushed before their ideas can breathe.

And for relationship people, jumping straight to problems feels harsh and disrespectful.

Roadblocks . . . crushed . . . harsh . . . disrespectful. What do all these words have in common? They're negative. And that's why your boss might think you're negative when you attempt to head off problems. And that's assuming you're always correct in your analysis—which of course, is unlikely.

Expert Insight: Marshall Goldsmith

Being perceived as negative can feel unfair, but in workplace conflict, building trust, and having more influence, perception matters. We had a great interview with the world's number one leadership coach, Marshall Goldsmith, author of *The Earned Life*.

When it comes to leadership, he said, "It doesn't matter what we said. All that matters is what they think they heard."[1]

Powerful Phrases When Your Boss Thinks You're Too Negative

Your manager and team need you to think through ideas and ensure the solutions you implement together are as sound as they can be. The shift away from being perceived as negative starts with connection.

"Wow, that's interesting . . ."

Find something interesting, fun, or positive about the idea and say that first. This connects you to the other person. Here are two more examples:

- "I appreciate you thinking about . . ."
- "That's a creative way of looking at this."

After affirming their idea, continue with something like:

"Here's how we can make sure this succeeds . . ."

This Powerful Phrase is critical. You will still share your challenges or concerns. But instead of stating them as problems, package them as solutions or opportunities.

For example, with your boss's idea of hiring a contractor, you might say:

"That's a great idea. Here are three things we can do to make sure it succeeds. First, let's ensure the contractor has experience in this technology. Then, if we can find someone at this price point without a contract-extension penalty and who has a team to back them up, this could really work."

Presenting your analysis as "ways to make this work" is magical. Your concerns don't come across as obstacles. You're contributing to the idea's success. When people hear what it will take to "make their idea work," they will form their own conclusions. They may propose follow-up solutions. Or they'll say, "That's a good point. I don't think this is the best idea." You didn't negate their idea, you supported it in a way that they could think it through.

"I want to make sure I give your idea the positive attention it warrants. Can we talk tomorrow morning?"

Use this Powerful Phrase when you know you're not at your best. If you're tired, frustrated, or tied in knots with other problems, you can pause and not respond right away. Taking responsibility for your state of mind and tone when you respond will help avoid the times where you're most likely to come across as negative.

Powerful Phrases When Your Boss Thinks You're Too Negative

 "Wow, that's interesting."

 "I appreciate you thinking about . . ."

 "That's a creative way of looking at this."

 "Here's how we can make sure this succeeds . . ."

 "I want to make sure I give your idea the positive attention it warrants. Can we talk tomorrow morning?"

V

COMMUNICATING WITH DIFFICULT PEOPLE

The Art of Wooing
the Weary and
Winning the Whiny

25

How to Deal With . . .
Lazy Coworkers

"It's okay to bring up these issues directly with your coworker.
Sometimes they just may not realize the impact they are having,
and a simple conversation can solve it."

—Female, 28, Canada

Scrolling social media. Long lunches. Arriving late.
Leaving early. "Phoning in" half-baked work. Constantly
hanging out by the coffee pot or in virtual chat rooms. Moving
slower than a sloth in a meditation retreat . . . There's not
much more annoying than a chronically lazy coworker.

It's easy to think, "Why in the world am I working so hard,
when this clown gets away with so much? Isn't my boss paying
attention?"

The tricky part of dealing with a lazy coworker is that it's
technically not your problem to solve. It's possible your manager is dealing with the issue and can't talk about it. But it's
also possible your manager is lazy or conflict avoidant.

Let's start with what not to do: don't adopt their bad habits.
Instead, concentrate on rocking your role and building a network of coworkers you admire and trust. Channel your frustration to ensure your performance stands out. The worst thing

you can do is slack on your work or standards. Your reputation will outlast the influence of this lazy coworker. Chapter 14 on team accountability could come in handy here too.

Next, don't engage in drama, complaining, or gossip about the lazy one. We've seen otherwise high-performing people waste more time complaining about the lazy coworker than the actual time the lazy person frittered away.

With these two "don'ts" in mind, here are Powerful Phrases to get curious with your coworker and escalate your concerns if necessary.

Powerful Phrases to Connect with a Lazy Coworker

Let's start with a few phrases to talk with the coworker directly. Your lazy coworker might feel overwhelmed or be dealing with something you don't fully understand.

"I've noticed you've been spending a lot of time on personal calls recently. Is everything okay?"

Of course, it's not your "job" to check in on a coworker. But if something is going on, that moment of curious kindness might be exactly what you both need.

"I'm worried about our team. Everyone's under so much stress. Can we talk about how we can best support one another and the team?"

These kinds of "we're all in the same boat" Powerful Phrases work well because you're inviting them to a collaboration conversation rather than making an accusation.

"Lately, I've been feeling like I'm taking on too much of the load. I'm curious about what this looks like from your perspective."

This one's a combination of clarity—clearly stating your concern, with a dose of curiosity.

"Hey, [name], can you give me a hand here?"

Sometimes a direct approach and invitation to partner with you can help your lazy coworker get moving.

Expert Insight: Alison Green

To some extent, the best approach depends on your relationship with your boss and what they're like. If you have a good relationship and they value directness over protocol, you might simply say: "Hey, I'm not sure if it's appropriate to raise this, but I'm concerned about how often Bob tries to get me to take on his work. I'm happy to help when it's needed, but I see him chronically spending an enormous amount of time socializing rather than working, and I feel like he wouldn't need my help if he focused on work more. **Can you give me advice about how to handle this?"**

Notice that this is couched in terms of asking for their advice on how you should handle it rather than you dumping it in their lap to handle. If he or she is a good boss, they are going to handle it themselves anyway—hopefully by paying more attention to how Bob is spending his time and addressing it with him if he or she sees that there's an issue. But by asking for their advice, you make it less about "tattling" and more about seeking his or her guidance.

—Alison Green, author of *Ask a Manager*
and the *Ask a Manager* blog

Powerful Phrases to Escalate a Lazy Coworker to Your Manager

If you've tried to talk with your coworker, and their lazy approach affects your performance, it might be time to make your manager aware of what's happening. Here are a few phrases that can help.

"I've noticed that [coworker's name] isn't contributing at the same level as the rest of us, and it's affecting our productivity and performance. I don't want to overstep my role here, but I want to ensure you are aware of the impact on the rest of the team."

Say this as a statement, so you don't put them on the spot for an immediate response. This approach also works because you're talking about the bigger impact on results, rather than just complaining about the person.

"Hey, boss. I've noticed we've had a few missed deadlines lately. My plate is already full, and I want to ensure our team meets our goals. Is there anything I can do in the short term to pitch in during this challenging time?"

You can do this without being a blamer or complainer. Resist the temptation to start with words like, "I know how lazy this dude is . . ." Instead, use this opportunity to make the conversation about you and how you can best help.

If your manager is aware of, and privately dealing with your lazy coworker, this phrase might be just perfect. But you don't want to use this one repeatedly if it turns out your manager's avoiding the accountability conversation.

The most important thing to remember when dealing with a lazy coworker is that your manager has formal responsibility.

Express your concern in terms of business outcomes and ensure your manager is aware. After that, your best approach is to focus on your work and invest in your productive relationships.

Powerful Phrases for Dealing with a Lazy Coworker

CONNECT WITH YOUR COWORKER

 "Is everything okay?"

 "Can we talk about how we can best support one another and the team?"

 "I've been feeling like I'm taking on too much of the load. I'm curious about what this looks like from your perspective."

 "Can you give me a hand here?"

TO ESCALATE TO YOUR MANAGER

 "I don't want to overstep my role here, but I want to ensure you are aware of the impact on the rest of the team."

 "Can you give me some advice on how to handle this?"

"Is there anything I can do to pitch in during the short run?"

26

How to Deal With . . .
Know-It-Alls

"You need to defend your point of view."

—Female, 24, Russia

If you turned straight to this chapter, you know the type: a coworker who thinks they know it all and doesn't hesitate to pontificate, question, and debate everything. They offer unsolicited advice or undesired help. These characters make you want to scream, "Stay in your lane!" or "Hey, I've got this!"

One of the frustrating aspects of dealing with a know-it-all is that sometimes they really do know a lot, but their (often unsolicited) advice is hard to take because they're so freaking arrogant. And sometimes what's coming across as "knowing it all" is really an insecure person's attempt to cover up what they don't know. Either way, showing up connected and curious is a good place to start.

When I (Karin) was in my late twenties with a newly earned graduate degree and a chance to finally work in HR at a Fortune 20 company, my job was to build high-performing teams. A few months in, I realized that the motivational theories I studied in grad school had not fully prepared me for navigating a complex organization in a constant firestorm of change and messy political dynamics. I was fighting a steep learning curve, and most days the curve won.

I spent more money than I could afford on a couple of decent suits and read every book on executive presence I could get my hands on. Every time I faced a new problem at work, I looked it up in my textbooks. I wanted to show up as polished as I could on the outside to compensate for the insecurity on the inside.

I shared my expertise in every meeting so I "wouldn't look dumb." Then one day, Dolores, my peer with two decades of experience, took me aside and asked me, "Do you know what Bob is saying about you? To *everyone?*"

Bob was a gregarious, old-school operations guy. If anyone could influence everyone, it was Bob. "What?" I braced myself to hear what I was sure was the laundry list of political missteps I made or judgment calls that backfired.

"He's telling everyone that you are the golden child. That everyone better watch their backs. I believe his exact words were, 'You've been brought in as an expert who is kicking ass and taking names.'"

Watching the incredulous look on my face, she smiled: "I know, it's funny—you're just a well-meaning, clumsy kid. Karin, if you're smart, you'll let Bob see behind the scenes of your struggle and ask for his help. Stop trying so hard to make a good impression and tell him you need advice."

That meeting with Bob was one of the best returns on any cup of coffee I've ever sipped (it's hard to beat the return on investment of a good coffee conversation). Bob needed to know that I knew I didn't know it all. He listened carefully and offered to help—and stopped his verbal sabotage. Eventually, he even endorsed some of my key initiatives.

Many of the know-it-alls we heard about in our research were more like clumsy Karin in the Dolores days—oversharing anything they know as a cover for what they don't.

Other know-it-alls know quite a bit. Sometimes their questions are spot-on. Often, they really want to help. A know-it-all can challenge you to think more deeply. When you know your office know-it-all is in the room, you might even anticipate the questions they'll ask, double-check your data, and prepare your response.

Powerful Phrases for Dealing with a Know-It-All

How can you show up with confidence and find your voice while also benefiting from their expertise? Bring in your Powerful Phrases.

POWERFUL PHRASES FOR HELPING A KNOW-IT-ALL UNDERSTAND THE IMPACT OF THEIR APPROACH

It's possible that your know-it-all doesn't understand the impact they're having. Like we saw with Dolores, sometimes a gentle conversation to point out the behavior and impact can make an enormous difference.

"I'm sure your intentions are good. And sometimes, when you tell me what to do, it makes me feel you question my expertise."

Assuming good intentions softens the conversation and is likely to make them more receptive to what you have to say next. Assuming, of course, you're following all the tone and manner tips we discussed in chapter 5. It's a clarity statement about the impact their behavior is having on you. We've seen this one work like magic for the know-it-all who really is just trying to be helpful.

"How do you think that went? (Pause for response.) What did you notice about the others in the room?"

You can adapt this curiosity Powerful Phrase to any circumstance where know-it-all behavior surfaces. If they're truly clueless about the impact of their behavior, they might think everything is great, and you'll need to probe some more. It's also quite possible they sensed something was wrong but can't put their finger on it. Show up with genuine curiosity and take the conversation from there.

"I've noticed that sometimes you dominate the conversation and others seem to shut down. For example, _____."

This Powerful Phrase is another clarity phrase that sets you up for a follow-up probe, such as "What's going on?" We talk more about this noticing, probing combo in chapter 14, where we share our I.N.S.P.I.R.E. Method for accountability conversations. If you love this approach, jump back and review the method.

Expert Insight: Virg Palumbo

A timeless rite of passage in the Marine Corps happens when an inexperienced, idealistic lieutenant who recently graduated warfare training has the first meeting with their seasoned platoon sergeant. Over three decades of leadership experience, my experience as the inexperienced lieutenant was the first of many similar encounters in my professional career.

More than likely, you are not checking into an infantry battalion, but human nature is human nature. Going into this meeting,

I received sage advice for this type of conversation: "You have two ears, two eyes, and one mouth. Use them in proportion."

We began our relationship with a conversation focused on the platoon sergeant's perspective, then built a common goal. Being consistent in our approach through moments of intensity, we could coordinate, communicate implicitly, establish role clarity, develop commonality in organizational vision, achieve common goals, and capitalize on each other's strengths as we built a world-class fighting organization.

ACTA NON VERBA (ACTIONS, NOT WORDS)

Your actions will define you. While Powerful Phrases will set the stage, your follow-up actions will add creditability or erode the partnership. As with most endeavors in life, there is no neutral in relationship building—each day it gets better or worse.

POWERFUL PHRASES

- "If you were in my shoes, what would be your focus?"
- "What do you think our team strengths are? Where do you think we can improve?"
- "How do you like to communicate?"
- "What are items you would like to see stopped? Items you would like to keep? Items to start?"

—Virg Palumbo, president, Organizational Efficiency, Kforce, captain, United States Marine Corps (93–99)

POWERFUL PHRASES TO HELP MANAGERS GET MORE VOICES INTO THE ROOM

If you're a manager with a know-it-all team member, they can suck the conversational oxygen out of the room (and in virtual meetings, it's even harder for others to get into a conversation). But to make the best decisions, you need every voice and perspective in the conversation.

"I could really use your help to draw others into the conversation. Do you think you could help me do that?"

One way to include every voice is to take your know-it-all aside and invite them to help draw other voices into the conversation. You can set this one up by first acknowledging their expertise. **"I know you're an expert here, and I could use your help."** You preserve their ego and get them to stop dominating the conversation.

"I want to ensure we hear from everyone, so I'm going to set the timer for five minutes and give everyone the same time to speak."

Don't overuse this one, but it's a great way to create a norm of proving the point that others have something important to say.

POWERFUL PHRASES TO SHARE YOUR EXPERTISE

Sometimes you need to stand your ground and share your expertise. These Powerful Phrases can help you redirect the conversation and politely make it clear to your know-it-all that you aren't in the market for their help or advice.

"I really appreciate your help, but I've got this."

This clarity phrase is blunt and effective.

"I've been working on this for quite some time, and I'm confident in this approach (or decision)."

This confident clarity statement is a bit more subtle than the previous one, but also gives you an opportunity to assert your expertise.

"We need to move quickly on this, so I'm going to make the call."

This one can work wonders if, in fact, you're the one who owns the decision.

How you approach the conversation with your know-it-all will vary based on your relationship and their receptivity. Give yourself the best chance for success by showing up with positive intentions (a strong desire to be helpful to them and collaborate). Be confident in your expertise and curious about what's happening for them.

Powerful Phrases When Dealing with a Know-It-All

HELP A KNOW-IT-ALL UNDERSTAND THEIR IMPACT

 "I'm sure your intentions are good. And sometimes, when you tell me what to do, it makes me feel like you question my expertise."

 "How do you think that went? What did you notice about the others in the room?"

 "I've noticed that sometimes you dominate the conversation. For example, . . ."

 "If you were in my shoes, what would be your focus?"

 "What do you think our team strengths are? Where do you think we can improve?"

"How do you like to communicate?"

 "What are items you would like to see stopped? Items you would like to keep? Items to start?"

GET MORE VOICES INTO THE ROOM

 "I could really use your help to draw others into the conversation. Do you think you could help me do that?"

 "I know you're an expert here, and I could use your help."

 "I want to ensure we hear from everyone, so I'm going to set the timer . . ."

SHARE YOUR EXPERTISE

 "I really appreciate your help, but I've got this."

 "I've been working on this for quite some time, and I'm confident in this approach/decision."

 "We need to move quickly on this, so I'm going to make the call."

27

How to Deal With . . .
Chronic Complainers

"Do not engage in drama."

—Female, 20, Singapore

When you're dealing with a chronic complainer, you might think, "Oh, I have a Powerful Phrase, 'Shut the f*** up and get back to work.'" Although that might feel cathartic, you have better options. Before we get to those, let's talk about Phil.

I (David) was about to start a daylong workshop at a large engineering firm when the HR director pulled me aside and said, "I've got to warn you about Phil. He's bad."

"What does 'bad' look like?" I asked.

"He is so cynical and complained so much during yesterday's session that the facilitator quit at the break halfway through the program."

Whoa. Complainers have that effect on people. They can suck the life out of you and your team and make everyone want to quit. Fortunately, Powerful Phrases can be very helpful with this workplace conflict. (And if *you* often get feedback that you're too negative or complain too much, be sure to check out chapter 24.)

Powerful Phrases for a Complainer Who's Never Happy

Let's talk about two types of chronic complainers. One is the person who's just never happy. Let's call him "Mr. Whiny." Mr. Whiny can be at a five-star resort with someone massaging his fingers with coconut oil and he'll find something to complain about. "It's too hot in here. I can hear you breathing. This coconut oil smells too much like coconut." Nothing is truly wrong, concerning, or threatening. Mr. Whiny complains because it somehow makes him feel better.

Chronic complainers like Mr. Whiny can be a huge drain on your time and energy. You can use Powerful Phrases to address the behavior and disengage from unproductive discussions.

"In the last hour, I've heard you mention that you're unhappy about when we're meeting, the decision we must make, and the meeting software we're using. What's going on?"

Use a neutral, nonjudgmental, curious tone here. When you call attention to the behavior of someone you suspect is an "I'm never happy" chronic complainer, they'll often tone it down. With this approach, you genuinely check to see if there's a problem. You're not ignoring them, but neither are you amping up their negative energy. If there's something legitimate in their grumbling, you can listen, reflect to connect (GOAT #11), and try to move them to act.

"That does sound frustrating. Do you want to make it better?"

This Powerful Phrase helps you know if you're talking to a Mr. Whiny. If they answer, "Yes, I want to make it better," then skip ahead to the next section of this chapter for phrases to continue the conversation. But if they defer and say something like, "Nah, it's not worth it. Nothing ever changes," then it's time to end the conversation.

"That's tough. Well, I'm up against a deadline here and must get back to it. Hope you have a better day."

You can't care more than they do. If they're not invested in doing anything differently, it's time to extract yourself from the conversation.

Powerful Phrases for Dealing with Chronic Complainers Who Care

Another common type of chronic complainer is someone who genuinely cares about the team and the work you do, but it's hard to see that caring because it's hidden under a veneer of cynicism. Let's call this caring complainer Ms. Cares a Lot. As you prepare to deal with Ms. Cares a Lot, it helps to understand what's happening for her. Some people have a naturally cautious or self-protective way of approaching life. It's kept them safe or avoided disaster (or at least feels that way).

If you tell Ms. Cares that they're being negative or a complainer, they'll respond honestly, "No, I'm not. I'm trying to prevent a problem, avoid needless frustration, and keep us on track." And her analytic, skeptical way of looking at things can be a real asset as you make decisions. The challenge is to help caring chronic complainers add that value without dragging you down in a vortex of cynicism.

Besides understanding their general approach, it's also helpful to understand where the "chronic" part comes from. When someone who cares complains frequently, it's often because they don't feel heard. People dismiss them as "negative" and roll their eyes. And the complainer's skepticism gets worse. A few Powerful Phrases can help redirect that energy to more positive outcomes. Curiosity and connection will work wonders.

"It sounds like you're concerned about . . ."

When your complainer raises an issue, avoid the temptation to shut them down. Use this Powerful Phrase to check for understanding (yes, yet another variation of GOAT #11—it's a GOAT for a reason!). If they're really worked up, grab a pen and paper and start writing what they say. Just the act of taking them seriously eases some of the pressure that's built up for them.

"And what else?"

This is a truly Powerful Phrase when talking to a caring complainer. You've listened intently. You've written what they said. Now, when you ask, "And what else?" it creates a pause. A moment of reflection. It gets them out of the autopilot "no one ever listens, so I'll keep talking" mode and gets them thinking critically about the issue. If there is more, listen and take notes. You might need one more "And what else" before they get out all their concerns.

Expert Insight: Oscar Trimboli

Listening is the willingness to have your mind changed.

—Oscar Trimboli, author of *How to Listen: Discover the Hidden Key to Better Communication*

"What do you see as the consequences if . . . ?"

This Powerful Phrase helps both of you get perspective. Sometimes your complainer will answer this question with, "Hmm, I guess the consequences aren't all that big, really." And they're ready to move on. But when they see significant concerns, you can continue with this question:

"What would it feel like if we could solve for that?"

Chronic complainers have been cynical for so long that it's sometimes hard for them to envision life improving. When you invite them to consider how it would feel, it opens the door to solutions.

"How do you think we can address this?"

With this Powerful Phrase, you shift the conversation to solutions. They may have a few and you can explore them together.

"If you could snap your fingers and create a solution, what would you like to see happen?"

For a caring complainer who isn't sure what to do, one way to break the impasse is with a question that helps them imagine change. Their solution might not be immediately practical, but it gives them a place to either take action or understand that the situation isn't as bad as they thought.

"It sounds like you want to . . ."

As you recap the conversation, focus on what action they want to take next. (And if they truly couldn't come up with a practical way forward, you might suggest monitoring the situation for a month and seeing if anything changes.)

"I'm glad we had this conversation . . ."

At some point, you need to help the caring complainer get moving (and get back to your work). This Powerful Phrase emphasizes that you've "had"—past tense—the conversation. You might need to pair it with a follow-up "I need to get back to . . ."

It turned out that Phil wasn't nearly as troublesome as the HR director feared. He had genuine, valid concerns. After listening to his questions and giving him truthful answers (even when they weren't always the answers he wanted), Phil became an advocate for the program. And you'll be able to help your chronic complainers too when you use these Powerful Phrases and genuinely listen.

Powerful Phrases for Dealing with Chronic Complainers

FOR COMPLAINERS WHO ARE NEVER HAPPY

 "I've heard you mention that you're unhappy about . . . and . . . and . . . What's going on?"

"That does sound frustrating. Do you want to make it better?"

"That's tough. Well, I'm up against a deadline here and must get back to it. Hope you have a better day."

FOR COMPLAINERS WHO CARE

"It sounds like you're concerned about . . ."

 "And what else?"

 "What do you see as the consequences if . . . ?"

"What would it feel like if we could solve for that?"

 "How do you think we can address this?"

"If you could snap your fingers and create a solution, what would you like to see happen?"

 "It sounds like you want to . . ."

 "I'm glad we had this conversation . . ."

28

How to Deal With . . .
Bullies

"Looking back, I feel I should have stood up for myself and not given in to this bully. I only feared hurting her and not getting into an ugly argument. However, this has made me not decide so many things for myself, like my career path, my job, etc., . . . at that time. I am much stronger now and would deal with such a bully differently if history was to repeat."

—Female, 47, Dubai

You shouldn't have to deal with a workplace bully. When you face truly toxic bullying behaviors, be prepared: your most Powerful Phrase might not work on the bully, and you may need to save your words for HR. With that said, most times, a well-articulated Powerful Phrase may be just the ticket to turn the situation around.

Sadly, stories about bullies were rampant in our research. The situations that ended well had two themes in common. First, the bullied person didn't face the situation alone. And second, they didn't react in the moment but planned a careful intervention with careful words.

"Fred's" Story (Now a CEO)

I was working on a project, and another guy made a mistake. But his boss thought it was my fault and left me a scathing voicemail—which he copied to six other people on the team. He got really personal in the attacks. I was new to this position. And, even if I had made a mistake, it was a horrible way to behave—so demeaning.

I was visibly upset, so I went to a conference room and called one of my colleagues and told them, "**I could really use your help** to process what just happened." This was a big deal for me. I'm not usually that vulnerable. Being able to reach out to someone when I wouldn't do that under normal circumstances meant the world.

I brought the team of people together, including the guy who had made the mistake. And in a moment of assertiveness, I didn't think I had in me, I said, **"Look, is this the way we're going to work together?** Where we blame each other and yell at each other and use public humiliation?" I was so frustrated—and I found my voice that day.

The intervention worked. It was a declaration that I wasn't the one to mess with. I think the best way to deal with a workplace bully is to be direct, strong, and professional. You can't let them get away with that behavior, even if you're in the junior position. With sloppy bullies like this, your dignity and strength are embarrassing to them. And it makes them look all the worse in front of anyone witnessing it. They're less likely to mess with you in the future.

"Is this the way we're going to work together?" is an excellent example of confronting a bully without confronting the person. It's a clarity phrase that describes the current and future situation.

Powerful Phrases for Dealing with a Workplace Bully

Here are some time-tested recommendations to confront bullies, bring clarity to the relationship, and put a stop to their behavior.

"That's not okay."

Saying "that's not okay" sends a clear message that you won't tolerate their bullying and that you expect them to treat you with respect. Sure, it's scary to confront a meanie. But you have the right to a safe workplace. By speaking up and setting boundaries, you take a powerful step toward protecting yourself and creating a more positive work environment for everyone.

"Nope, I can't let you talk to me that way."

A close cousin to "That's not okay" is "Nope. I can't let you talk to me that way."

"I would like to discuss this issue with you in a private setting."

You can also create clarity about where and when you will engage. Many workplace bullies love to perform for a crowd. By saying, "I would like to discuss this issue with you in a private setting," you take control of the situation and remove the bully's audience.

If the bully refuses the private meeting, you can then follow up with, **"I would prefer to have this conversation privately, but . . ."** and then add one or more of the other Powerful Phrases in this chapter. For example: **"I would prefer to have this conversation privately, but if you prefer to do it here, we will. What just happened there is not okay. I am happy to** have robust discussions and disagreements when we can do it without name-calling or insults."

"I will not engage in this behavior."

Another way to create clarity is to be clear about your behavior. Workplace bullies often try to provoke others into a reaction. By saying, "I will not engage in this behavior," you refuse to play into their game and assert your right to be treated with respect. This phrase communicates they will not bully you into reacting.

"I will be happy to _____, when _____."

This is another version of creating clarity about your behavior. For example, "I will be happy to (have this conversation), when (we can do it without name-calling)." Defining your behavior restores your power—the same power a bully tries to steal.

"I would like to involve HR in this discussion."

When nothing else works, this Powerful Phrase is vital. By saying, "I would like to involve HR in this discussion," you clarify the situation is serious. You're communicating that you will not tolerate being bullied and that you will take action to protect yourself and the team.

"Lilly's" Story (Now a Successful Entrepreneur)

My company was acquired into a very different culture and leadership style. There were so many tangly problems "collaborating" as we began working together. One result of the collaboration failures is that I received critical materials for a presentation a few minutes before I needed to present—at the client site—to our C-suite sponsors.

So, I'm updating our presentation deck (high-stress mode, because in moments I'm going to be the presenter, ready or not!) with part of the client team in the conference room. My new CEO is there. As I'm racing to get this done, he's growling negative feedback (targeted at me) about the presentation and shaking his head to emphasize his disappointment. He was making everyone uncomfortable and setting exactly the wrong mood. And it was too late for it to be remotely constructive.

I waited a week to soften the emotional impact. Then I set up a call with my CEO and a project manager from his team (someone he trusted) that had been in the room. I remained calm and explained, **"This is what it's like to be me in this situation."** I also explained my concerns about how the client might have felt watching it happen.

I also successfully debunked some of the criticisms he'd given that I hadn't wanted to argue about with clients in the room.

Initially, he downplayed his behavior and denied that there were clients in the room while it was happening—but his project manager confirmed everything. My CEO took a long breath. He said, "It took great maturity and discipline for you to wait for the proper moment and environment to give me this feedback. **Thank you.**"

That conversation didn't save the project, but it built more trust between the two of us. I'm not taking all the credit. The

CEO's response to this conversation was much more considered and strategic than his feedback at the client site. From my perspective, the moral is that time, place, and company (who is there) all matter when you're having a challenging conversation with your boss.

Dealing with a workplace bully is never fun. And yet, quick action can prevent the situation from escalating. By using these Powerful Phrases, you can assert your boundaries and support a better workplace for others. Keep in mind that when you use these phrases, your actions need to match your words. You aren't making threats—you're defining what you will and won't do or accept. Be sure to follow through.

Powerful Phrases for Dealing with a Workplace Bully

"I could really use your help . . ."

"Is this the way we're going to work together?"

"That's not okay."

"Nope, I can't let you talk to me that way."

"I would like to discuss this issue with you in a private setting."

"I will not engage in this behavior."

"I will be happy to _____, when _____."

"I would like to involve HR in this discussion."

"This is what it's like to be me in this situation."

29

How to Deal With . . .
Workplace Gossips

"Go straight to the source and talk about the situation. Cut the rumor by the root."

—Female, 26, Mexico

I f you're dealing with workplace gossip, let's get you some help. In today's digital reality, workplace gossip can travel fast and be hard to unwind. The good news is, like the credit stealers in chapter 19, Powerful Phrases work well to stop workplace gossip. Most people understand that gossip is not helpful, and pointing out their behavior is often enough to make it stop.

"I know this isn't funny. But you must admit, it kind of is." My (Karin's) executive assistant said with a big grin. "You should probably know the rumor that's going around about you." I wasn't quite prepared for the absurdity of the workplace gossip that followed.

"You're a lipstick lesbian planning a secret getaway to Jamaica with 'Laura' (not her real name)." Laura was one of the few female direct reports on my new team. Now, to be fair, Laura and I both wear lipstick. So, there's that. And we spent a good bit of time together because of her pivotal role on the team.

But we were not in love (with each other). And neither of us was headed to Jamaica any time soon. Although in retrospect, a minute on the beach might have been a pleasant relief from dealing with the pressures of a new team I hadn't yet won over. If I had gone to Jamaica, it would have been with a tween and a toddler in tow. And I probably would have forgotten to pack the lipstick.

The situation got dicier when HR investigated. That's when I gathered a few of the instigators and addressed the situation directly. "This isn't true. And I know you know that. What's going on here?" That was a pivotal moment for our relationship. I think my confident approach to their nonsense helped me gain their respect (and eventually, this team won awards for their extraordinary sales results).

Powerful Phrases for Dealing with Gossip

An effective way to de-escalate gossip is to stay poised and confident. The more rattled you appear, the more people may wonder if the rumor is true. Address the gossip head-on by sharing what you've heard, the gossip's impact, and ask for help to stop the destructive conversation. And if someone gossips about another person, you can usually stop them, or at least slow them down, by letting them know you don't engage in gossip. Then encourage them to talk directly to the person involved.

POWERFUL PHRASES TO USE HUMOR TO DEFLECT THE GOSSIP
For a ridiculous rumor, confidence and humor can lighten the mood. Here are a few of our favorites.

- "I heard there's a rumor circulating that
  _____. If that were a movie, I'd be

sure to buy a ticket. I hope whoever started this bit of workplace gossip is working on a screenplay."

- "So, apparently, I've been _____. I've got to say that rumor is a lot more interesting than how I actually spend my evenings."

Expert Insight: Bev Kaye

GRAIN OF TRUTH?

If the gossip is about you, ask yourself this difficult question: **"Is there a grain of truth in the unfair thing they've said?"** Is there something in your behavior that might lead them to start this particular rumor? An important part of navigating a successful career is understanding people's perspectives of how you show up. Even if their perceptions and words are unfair or inaccurate, it's better to know what people are "whispering in the hallways" so you can make informed choices of what to do next.

—Bev Kaye, best-selling author of *Love 'Em or Lose 'Em*
and *Help Them Grow or Watch Them Go*

POWERFUL PHRASES TO ASK FOR HELP WITH WORKPLACE GOSSIP

After showing up with confidence and a bit of humor, another powerful move is to ask for help. It's hard to keep gossiping after you just agreed to help.

"I've heard there's a rumor going around. What do you think I can do to help stop this unfair workplace gossip from spreading?"

You're not accusing them of anything, but you are addressing the rumor head-on and asking them for a specific solution.

"You know, I've been really working hard to _____. And what makes me sad is _____. Can you help me nip this in the bud?"

This Powerful Phrase is the perfect trifecta to reinforce your personal brand's positive aspects, show some humanity about how the rumor makes you feel, and ask for help.

"As you know, my reputation as a _____ is important to me. Why do you suppose people think this could be true?"

This one's helpful to get underneath the root cause of the gossip. Perhaps there was an action that was misinterpreted that you can clear up.

POWERFUL PHRASES TO STOP A RUMOR ABOUT A COWORKER

When the rumor is about someone else, here are a few productive ways to intervene. And no, we don't recommend you "mind your own business." Recall the advice from Liane Davey in chapter 2: "It's the witness—the one with some emotional distance—who has the best chance to intervene constructively."

"Does this conversation feel fair to you?"

The time to ask this question is when you're sure the answer is "no." This is a call to maturity and can go a long way in stopping the conversation before it can do additional harm.

"What if we called _____ (insert person whom the rumor is about) and asked for their perspective on this?"

The most destructive part about gossip is that it's about someone who's not in the room. This is another phrase that gets people to stop and think about what they're doing. It's also a subtle threat that you might let the other person in on what's going on.

"If someone were saying this about you, would you want me to tell you?"

Of course, the implied answer here is yes. And it's a way of saying, "If you don't stop, I'm going to let the victim of this gossip know what you're doing."

"Wow. I wouldn't want people talking about me like this behind my back."

This Powerful Phrase also works as a call to maturity and appropriate team norms.

FOR MANAGERS: WHAT TO SAY WHEN THE RUMOR IS TRUE (BUT NOT READY FOR DISCUSSION)

If you're a manager, sometimes you'll have confidential information that you can't discuss. These situations can feel dicey. Here are a few phrases to handle workplace gossip that's partially true.

"There's a lot we don't know about this. Rumors and gossip only make these kinds of situations worse. Let's wait until we know more."

In the absence of information, people often assume the worst.

"I know this is a stressful time, and I'll share more as soon as I can."

Here, you're asking your team to give it time.

"I've found in these circumstances the stories we make up in our minds are usually worse than what will happen. Let's wait and get the facts."

Like with the reflect-to-connect GOAT, you are acknowledging their feelings.

We get more of what we encourage and less of what we criticize or ignore. If you want to build a high-performing, human-centered team culture, it's worth the effort to stop the rumors and workplace gossip.

Powerful Phrases for Dealing with Workplace Gossip

USE HUMOR TO DEFLECT

 "I hope whoever started this bit of workplace gossip is working on a screenplay."

 "I've got to say that rumor is a lot more interesting than how I actually spend my evenings."

ASK FOR HELP

 "Is there a grain of truth in the unfair thing they've said?"

 "What do you think I can do to help stop this unfair workplace gossip from spreading?"

 "You know, I've been really working hard to _____. And what makes me sad is _____. Can you help me nip this in the bud?"

 "Why do you suppose people think this could be true?"

TO STOP A RUMOR ABOUT A COWORKER

"Does this conversation feel fair to you?"

"What if we called _____ (insert person whom the rumor is about) and asked for their perspective on this?"

"If someone were saying this about you, would you want me to tell you?"

"Wow. I wouldn't want people talking about me like this behind my back."

FOR MANAGERS: WHEN A RUMOR IS TRUE (BUT YOU CAN'T DISCUSS)

"There's a lot we don't know about this. I trust we'll learn more soon."

"Rumors and gossip only make these kinds of situations worse. Let's wait until we know more."

"I know this is a stressful time, and I'll share more as soon as I can."

"I've found in these circumstances the stories we make up in our minds are usually worse than what will happen. Let's wait and get the facts."

30

How to Deal With . . .
Idea Crushers

"Focus on the bigger picture. Remember that the ultimate goal is
to complete the project successfully. Keep this in mind when
discussing different ideas and solutions."

—Male 23, Russia

You've got a game-changing idea. Maybe it will make
things better for your customers or save everybody a ton
of time. So, what do you do when your teammates won't listen?
How do you get them to take your idea seriously?

You might find it weirdly comforting to remember that the
person you're trying to persuade is likely stressed or tired and
dealing with pressures they're not discussing (see chapter 1).
Even if your idea will make life easier, it still takes energy to
consider doing something different. Inertia is real. Get the
confidence to persevere through their resistance by connecting to *why* your idea matters and the *difference* that it will make.

And our hope for you is that you will keep trying. When
your peers are with you, it's more likely that your manager
will take the idea seriously. In our research for *Courageous
Cultures*, 67 percent said their manager operates around the
notion of "this is the way we've always done it." One of the best

ways to get your manager's attention is to get your coworkers behind it. So, rallying them around your idea is a great place to start.

Of course, advocating for your idea just might bring you satisfaction and even joy. When we ask participants in our strategic leadership and team innovation programs about courageous moments where they spoke up and persistently promoted their ideas, the words they use to describe their feelings after are remarkably consistent: "fantastic," "proud," "relieved," "excited," and "accomplished."

One quick point before we move to the Powerful Phrases: one of the best ways to get people to pay attention to *your* idea is to have a reputation for listening to *other people's* ideas. When someone brings you an idea, respond with the following:

"Interesting, I'd love to explore this with you."

If you want people to listen to your ideas, make it a habit to listen to theirs. When you have a reputation for caring about your peers and supporting them in their efforts, they're more likely to take you and your idea seriously.

Powerful Phrases for Dealing with an Idea Crusher

Now, let's move on to Powerful Phrases you can use when a coworker crushes your idea. When your coworker won't listen, begin your conversation with what matters most to them—both their immediate needs and their long-term goals. Here are a few examples:

- "I've found a work-around that could save us at least ten hours a week of wasted effort. Can I walk you through it?"

- "Would you be open to hearing my idea to dramatically reduce client frustration?"
- "I've figured out a way to stop our boss from micromanaging this project. Would you like to hear more?"

"Here's exactly how we can make this happen . . ."

When a coworker won't listen, maybe they're afraid of taking on more work. Show them you've thought through the idea and broken it down into small, tangible actions. Making it feel doable can help reduce feelings of overwhelm.

"If I were you, I'd be wondering . . ."

Anticipate and speak to your coworker's objections as early as possible. You're showing that you get them and care enough to think through what matters to them. That's powerful for building relationship and connection. Another variation on this Powerful Phrase is, **"I imagine you have some concerns about how to pull this off. I've given a great deal of thought to that and here's what I've come up with . . ."** Then list your concerns and how to overcome them.

Expert Insight: Mofoluwaso Ilevbare

I was on a team organizing the fifth global leadership conference for more than two thousand leaders from different countries. For weeks, we brainstormed, hoping to wow the audience in ways they had not experienced before.

I noticed that each time I brought up ideas, a colleague more experienced in organizing such events would quickly shut them down, claiming to know the audience's likes and dislikes. Before the next meeting, I scheduled some one-on-one time (I called it a coffee chat so it wouldn't sound formal).

While relaxing and having a good time, I brought up planning for the conference. I asked what he liked about the approach and his fears about some of my suggestions. As I listened, we painted an imaginary picture of what success would look like. We asked questions such as these:

- "What if we tried this or that?"
- "How about if we moved this to that?"
- "If we want to trigger a different response to that segment, how can we leverage the diversity in the group to bring more creative ideas to the table?"
- "How best can we work together to reach an outcome where everyone on the team feels heard and contributes fairly to the outcome?"

I shared examples of similar activities and how helpful they could be in getting the desired outcomes. Ultimately, we implemented the best event ever, and we remain buddies today.

—Mofoluwaso Ilevbare, confidence coach and chief people officer, Allied Pinnacle, Australia and New Zealand

"What have I missed?"

This Powerful Phrase works because it assumes there is something else and that you truly want to know what they think. If you've been thorough and thought through all their concerns, it also helps them see that you've covered everything.

"What do you think this costs us?"

The idea behind this Powerful Phrase is to have your colleague describe the consequences of inaction. People are more likely to buy into an idea when they feel ownership. Asking them to describe the problem gives them ownership of finding a solution. Some variations on this include the following:

- "How do you experience this challenge?"
- "How much time do you think we waste every week with this?"
- "What would a solution to this problem mean for you?"

"Here's the support I would need from you . . ."

After you've built connection through these Powerful Phrases, one of the best ways to help a coworker listen and engage with your idea is to have a clear "ask." What specifically are you asking for them to do? Are you looking for help to engage stakeholders? Do you need help with certain elements of the project? What specifically do you need done? Here are a few examples:

- "I'm thinking that if each of us spent (insert required time) this month, we could knock this out."
- "I hope you will help advocate for this with your manager. I've prepared some talking points."
- "I'm looking for a few customers to trial this with. Would you be open to that?"

Being able to collaborate well and get support for your ideas is a critical career-building skill. When you can connect at a human level, communicate your idea in terms that matter to them, talk through logistics, anticipate and address concerns, and know your "ask," you're considerably more likely to have your coworker take your idea seriously.

Powerful Phrases for Dealing with an Idea Crusher

"Interesting, I'd like to explore this with you."

"I've found a work-around that could save us . . . Can I walk you through it?"

"Would you be open to hearing my idea to dramatically reduce . . . ?"

"Here's exactly how we can make this happen."

"If I were you, I'd be wondering . . ."

"I imagine you have some concerns . . . Here's what I've come up with."

"What if we tried this or that?"

"How can we leverage . . . ?"

"How best can we work together to reach . . . ?"

"What have I missed?"

"What do you think this costs us?"

"How do you experience this challenge?"

"How much time do you think we waste every week with this?"

"What would a solution to this problem mean for you?"

"Here's the support I would need from you . . ."

"If each of us spent (required time) this month, we could . . ."

"I hope you will . . ."

"I'm looking for . . . Would you be open to that?"

31

How to Deal With . . .
Passive-Aggressive Coworkers

"Stay calm."

—Female, 23, Vietnam

P assive-aggressive behavior is one of the most contagious
forms of conflict. It's easy to let yourself react with frustration and be passive-aggressive (or aggressive-aggressive) yourself. Now you look like the jerk—not good.

Let's start with what we mean by "passive-aggressive" behavior. The aggressive part is that the person feels anger or hostil-
ity. The passive part is that they don't express anger directly.
Rather, the anger hides in underhanded behaviors of power,
control, or deception. For example, a passive-aggressive comment about being passive-aggressive might look like, "Oh, they
always seem to avoid taking responsibility for their actions. It
must be nice to live in a world where you're never wrong."

When you first confront someone who has passive-aggressive
habits, they often insist that everything's fine. Or that maybe
the problem is just in your head? (If that sounds like gaslighting, there are passive-aggressive forms of gaslighting, along

with the well-known overt form of manipulation and brain-washing.) Typical passive-aggressive behaviors include things like the following:

- Snarky comments
- Bitter, critical, or demeaning humor
- Withholding information
- Backhanded compliments
- Sabotaging your success by failing to meet a commitment

Powerful Phrases for Working with a Passive-Aggressive Colleague

Before we get to the phrases, let's get one "do not" out of the way: do not tell someone they're passive-aggressive. It doesn't work. They'll get defensive or accuse you of the same thing. After all, how dare you label me? Instead, get some space, stay calm, and use these phrases.

POWERFUL PHRASES TO ASK YOURSELF
"Is this a pattern?

All of us have moments where we're frustrated, don't know how to express our concerns, or are clumsy. If the specific situation is new, it's worth having some patience and seeing if there is a pattern of passive-aggressive behavior.

"Is this a big deal?"

If the passive-aggressive behavior is a minor issue, some-times ignoring it is the best way to go. But if they withheld information and made you look bad in front of the executive team, or this is the third time it happened, it's a big deal. You need to address the behavior.

POWERFUL PHRASES TO RAISE YOUR CONCERN

These phrases will help you bring up your concerns. Often, just drawing attention to the issues will help resolve them.

"I noticed that . . ."

One of the most powerful ways to address passive-aggressive behavior is to calmly describe what happened. Staying calm avoids playing into their game. Here are three examples:

- "I noticed during the meeting you said, 'It must be nice to be the favorite.'"
- "I noticed that in your presentation you included the data that showed your team's results in one category but did not include the other three."
- "I've noticed that you always cc my manager on all your emails to me and am curious what's happening there."

For someone who doesn't have deeply ingrained passive-aggressive behaviors, shining a light on what happened is often all it takes to put a stop to it. You'll know this person because they say something like, "Yeah, you're right. I was having a bad day" or "Hmm, good point. I shouldn't do that."

"What I hear you saying is . . ."

When a coworker says something snarky, uses critical humor, or some other passive-aggressive statement, it's usually because they're upset or frustrated. Once again, don't react to how they said it or even to what they said. Respond instead to what their words represent. This is a master-level check for understanding (GOAT #11). For example, **"What I hear you saying is that you feel like I'm getting more opportunities than I deserve. Is that right?"**

If you can say this calmly, and without judgment, you might start a meaningful, authentic conversation about what they think and feel. For example, they might agree: "Yeah, I'm frustrated. It seems like everything goes your way." Or they might disagree: "No, you definitely deserve the opportunities. I'm just frustrated that I'm not getting them too."

You've just unlocked the hidden emotion that they didn't know how to express—and helped them express it. From there, you might continue with a reflect-to-connect statement (see GOAT #3). Something like, "Yeah, it can be frustrating when everyone else seems to get the opportunities you want."

"How can I help?"

Wait, what? You want me to help the obnoxious, passive-aggressive person?

Well, maybe. If they shared their frustration, offering your support can build connection. It also gives them a chance to say directly if you've done anything that made the situation worse. You can take responsibility if you need to or look for ways to encourage or support them. In the best case, you've turned them into an ally. In the worst case, they won't have the same animosity and are more likely to leave you alone.

POWERFUL PHRASES TO FOCUS ON THE WORK

Sometimes, your best approach with a passive-aggressive coworker is to focus on specific goals or the facts of the situation.

"Here is what we're accountable for."

Use this one when you have a colleague who doesn't follow through on commitments and then claims "I forgot" or "I didn't think that was a full plan." Document everyone's commitments and give everyone involved a copy. You'll help the team get things done and remove the passive-aggressive person's opportunity to make excuses.

"This is what happened/what I've done/what the data says. You can look here."

When someone passive-aggressively misrepresents the facts, calmly repeat the truth, and invite people to examine the facts for themselves. For example, you might say, "It sounds like there's a misunderstanding here. I completed these reports, submitted them, and finance approved them. Here they are if it would be helpful to review."

"I really want to make this work, and I need your help."

This is a Powerful Phrase to use with a third party—possibly your manager or human resource representative. When you address the person and the pattern continues, take time to document the specific instances, including dates, times, and what happened. Then ask for help.

Approach the situation with humility. For example, you might tell your manager, **"I'm committed to the team and to making this work. My coworker's actions here are affecting my ability to do my work, but I'm not having any luck addressing it. I need your help."** (Humility and diplomacy are vital when you talk with your manager. They might not be close enough to the situation to understand. Or the passive-aggressive person might have ingratiated themself with the boss to avoid accountability.)

Expert Insight: Amy Gallo

You can't avoid passive-aggressive people.

They're in practically every workplace, and even great colleagues sometimes act passive-aggressively. We all do. I know I have resorted to this behavior at times myself. I'm not proud, but it's true. Your coworker (or you!) behaves passive-aggressively when they're not forthcoming about what they're thinking or feeling. Instead, they use indirect methods to express themselves.

They might roll their eyes or give you the cold shoulder, but when you ask what's wrong, they say, "Nothing," implying it's all in your head.

Acting like this doesn't make someone a bad person. In fact, passive-aggression often comes from a very tender, human place:

- A fear of failure and/or desire to be perfect
- A fear of rejection and/or desire to be liked
- A fear of conflict and/or a desire for harmony
- A fear of being powerless or lacking influence and/or a desire for control

Most of the time, your colleague is not being a jerk on purpose. And if you can understand a little about what motivates their behavior, your relationship can be a lot less painful.

—Amy Gallo, author of *Getting Along:*
How to Work with Anyone (Even Difficult People)

Most passive-aggressive behavior happens because the person doesn't know how to get what they need in a more direct way. Addressing the behavior calmly and directly can help defuse the conflict. It's not your job to change the other person (and you can't even if you wanted to). But with these Powerful Phrases, you can improve the relationship and sometimes gain a colleague.

Powerful Phrases for Working with a Passive-Aggressive Colleague

ASK YOURSELF

 "Is this a pattern?"

 "Is this a big deal?"

RAISE YOUR CONCERN

 "I noticed that . . ."

 "What I hear you saying is . . ."

 "How can I help?"

FOCUS ON THE WORK

 "Here is what we're accountable for."

 "This is what happened/what I've done/what the data says. You can look here."

 "I really want to make this work, and I need your help."

How to Deal With . . .
Difficult Customers

"One of the biggest and most memorable conflicts I had at work was when I disagreed with my manager on how to handle a customer service issue. My manager wanted to take a more aggressive approach to resolving the issue, while I felt that a more diplomatic approach would be more beneficial in the long run. We ended up compromising and taking a moderate approach to the situation, which ended up being successful."

—Male, 25, United States

I f you've worked with customers for more than a minute, you know that the adage "The customer is always right" just isn't true. Which is what makes communicating with them so challenging. Your job is to make things right, but you can't possibly please all the people all the time.

I've (Karin) led tens of thousands of customer-facing employees over the years, including managing more contact center and retail customer escalations than I'd care to admit. And with all that experience, there's one thing I can say with absolute confidence: it's statistically unlikely that the difficult customer you're dealing with woke up this morning, brushed their teeth, and thought, "You know what might be fun to do today? Let's make calls or visit stores and be as difficult as possible. I'm gonna stir up some trouble."

And yet, according to the ACA State of Customer Service and CX, 32 percent of us admit to having yelled at a customer service agent. In fact, most would rather not even have to call. Thirty-eight percent of Americans said they'd rather clean a toilet than call customer service.[1] These scary screamers are likely reasonable human beings most of the time. But the fact that they had to call in the first place means something's gone wrong. By the time they got through the self-serve, half-baked AI bots and a few inane, circular transfers, they unleash their compounded frustration on the first human who will listen. You.

We get it. Some customers are jerks. (We will not be calling these difficult customers "Karens" for obvious reasons.) The majority are more like you—doing the best they can to get through a tough day. What do they all have in common? A genuine need to be seen and heard. That's where your Powerful Phrases come in.

Powerful Phrases When Dealing with a Difficult Customer

Start with connection and end with a firm commitment. From the very start, your customer needs to feel you understand them and their concern and that you have the expertise and desire to fix their issue.

"I'm so sorry this happened to you. Let's fix this right now."

A good start is always "I'm sorry" and acknowledging their concern and emotion.

"I'm sure that's incredibly frustrating. That's certainly not the experience we want you to have working with us."

Simple statements like these help the customer feel seen, de-escalate emotions, and set the tone for a productive dialogue. Even if the customer accidentally drove their car through your storefront plate-glass display, you can still express sympathy. (This rates high in the "weirdest calls I've ever received" category: "Karin, we've got a Honda wrapped around the iPad display. Thankfully, no one is hurt.") You're not sorry for their mistake, you're empathizing with their circumstance.

"I know exactly what we need to do next" and "I'm on it. I'm not letting you go until we get this resolved."

Building the customer's confidence in the first forty seconds of the interaction is another great way to calm a concerned customer. This Powerful Phrase infuses confidence into the conversation and reassures the customer that you care.

Expert Insight: Shep Hyken

FIVE-STEP PROCESS FOR DEALING WITH DIFFICULT CUSTOMERS

Customer experience expert and *New York Times* best-selling author Shep Hyken shares five simple steps for dealing with difficult customers:

1. Acknowledge the complaint
2. Apologize to the customer
3. Fix what needs to get fixed
4. Own it
5. Do it with urgency

"Is that a puppy I hear in the background? Does she chew up the underwear in your laundry basket?"

You want to be curious about their circumstances, experiences, frustrations, and even the cues you're picking up in the background. Note: This question will either immediately de-escalate the conversation or make it worse as they see it as an attempt to change the subject, so pay attention to the cues.

"Let me be sure I have this right: (summarize). What details did I miss that are important for me to understand?"

Especially if your customer has explained their story to someone else, this step is vital. This check for understanding serves two purposes. First, the customer feels heard. And second, it helps ensure you don't miss vital information.

"What would a successful outcome look like for you?"

This Powerful Phrase clarifies what's really on their minds. Even if you can't meet that expectation, it's better to know what they want.

"Here's what I'm going to do next. And I'm going to follow up with you tomorrow and ensure we resolve the situation."

Be sure to use this Powerful Phrase for commitment. After all, the follow-through is what your customer cares about most. What are you going to do next, by when, and how will they know?

As you can see, all four dimensions come in handy when dealing with difficult customers. Begin with connection, then clarify the situation and your expertise as quickly as possible. Get curious about the circumstances and the best ways to resolve their concern. And close with a confident commitment.

Powerful Phrases for Dealing with a Difficult Customer

 "I'm so sorry this happened to you. Let's fix this right now."

 "I'm sure that's incredibly frustrating. That's certainly not the experience we want you to have working with us."

 "I know exactly what we need to do next."

 "I'm on it. I'm not letting you go until we get this resolved."

 "Is that a puppy I hear in the background? Does she chew up the underwear in your laundry basket?"

 "Let me be sure I have this right . . . What details did I miss that are important for me to understand?"

 "What would a successful outcome look like for you?"

 "Here's what I'm going to do next . . ."

 "I'm going to follow up with you tomorrow and ensure we resolve the situation."

You've Got This

You've got this. Not because you now have hundreds of Powerful Phrases to use. Not because you'll get all the words just right. You've got this because you care enough to work at it. You wouldn't have read this book if your relationships, influence, and results didn't matter.

Caring is contagious. You build relationships one care-filled sentence at a time.

Each time you connect or clarify expectations, you make the next conversation easier. When you're consistently curious, you have more information to make wiser choices. Plus, a beautiful side effect of curiosity is that it inspires other people to be more curious too. Which makes everyone smarter. And when you're clear about commitments, the next conversation is way easier—for everybody.

Mastering conflict takes practice. Your conversations may feel awkward at first or not work the way you hoped. But that conversation is still a win. You embraced growth and took a significant step forward. So, we'll leave you with these last four Powerful Phrases to inspire your journey:

- "What have I learned about myself through this interaction?"

- "What have I learned about another person?"
- "When I think about how I showed up for the conversation, what brings me the most pride?"
- "What advice would I give myself if I face this conflict again?"

When we ask participants in our programs how they feel after having an important difficult conversation, the word they use most frequently is "and":

- "Nervous *and* relieved."
- "Stressed *and* grateful."
- "Kind of freaked out *and* amazed by the outcomes."

You're headed toward some beautiful "ands."

Notes

CHAPTER 1

1. Morgan, Kate. "The Search for Meaning at Work." BBC, September 7, 2022. https://www.bbc.com/worklife/article/20220902-the-search-for-meaning-at-work.

2. World Health Organization: WHO. "COVID-19 Pandemic Triggers 25% Increase in Prevalence of Anxiety and Depression Worldwide." World Health Organization, March 2, 2022. Accessed June 28, 2023. https://www.who.int/news/item/02-03-2022-covid-19-pandemic-triggers-25-increase-in-prevalence-of-anxiety-and-depression-worldwide.

3. GSDRC. "Conflict, Social Change and Conflict Resolution. An Enquiry—GSDRC." GSDRC—Governance, Social Development, Conflict and Humanitarian Knowledge Services, September 4, 2015. https://gsdrc.org/document-library/conflict-social-change-and-conflict-resolution-an-enquiry/.

4. Southern Poverty Law Center. "White Nationalist," n.d. https://www.splcenter.org/fighting-hate/extremist-files/ideology/white-nationalist?gclid=CjwKCAjwvpCkBhB4EiwAujULMu-ek7hfQilh4bSPdNDm8ejQM0reKvRk2aVRt2WiM-OEb0Rbbydz1BoC7GcQAvD_BwE.

5. NOAA Climate.gov. "Climate Change: Global Temperature," January 18, 2023. https://www.climate.gov/news-features/understanding-climate/climate-change-global-temperature.

6. For more: https://www.shrm.org/resourcesandtools/tools-and-samples/toolkits/pages/managingworkplaceconflict.aspx.

7. Hari, Johann. *Stolen Focus: Why You Can't Pay Attention—and How to Think Deeply Again.* Crown, 2022.

CHAPTER 2

1. Buckingham, Marcus, and Ashley Goodall. "Why Feedback Rarely Does What It's Meant To." *Harvard Business Review,*

March 10, 2023, http://hbr.org/2019/03/the-feedback
-fallacy.

CHAPTER 4

1. The Myers-Briggs Company. "Conflict at Work: A Research
    Report." The Myers-Briggs Company: Sunnyvale, CA, August
    2022. https://www.themyersbriggs.com/en-US/Programs
    /Conflict-at-Work-Research.
2. Edmondson, Amy C. *The Fearless Organization: Creating
    Psychological Safety in the Workplace for Learning, Innovation, and
    Growth.* John Wiley & Sons, 2018.
3. Sheen, Martin. "Martin Sheen: 4 Pieces of Advice for the Next
    Generation." *Time,* August 26, 2016. https://time.com/4465252
    /martin-sheen-we-days/.

CHAPTER 5

1. Yang, Qiwei, Deyu Hu, Jianfeng Wang, and Yan Wu. "Processing
    Facial Expressions That Conflict with Their Meanings to an
    Observer: An Event Related Potential Study." *Frontiers in
    Psychology* 11 (June 17, 2020). https://doi.org/10.3389/fpsyg
    .2020.01273.

CHAPTER 10

1. "Human Workplace Index: The Price of Invisibility," February 3,
    2023. https://www.workhuman.com/resources/human
    -workplace-index/human-workplace-index-the-price-of
    -invisibility.
2. OpenAI's ChatGPT AI language model, response to question
    from authors, April 7, 2023.

CHAPTER 14

1. So much research points to this. If you like reading it firsthand,
    take a look at Google's Project Aristotle and the emphasis on
    Dependability: https://www.nytimes.com/2016/02/28
    /magazine/what-google-learned-from-its-quest-to-build-the
    -perfect-team.html. For a more academic treatment and the

importance of relationships in accountability: https://link
.springer.com/article/10.1007/s10551-021-04969-z.

CHAPTER 19

1. "Bad Boss Index: 1,000 Employees Name Worst Manager
   Behaviors," n.d. https://www.bamboohr.com/blog/bad
   -boss-index-the-worst-boss-behaviors-according-to-employees
   -infographic.

CHAPTER 24

1. Dye, David. "The Earned Life with Marshall Goldsmith."
   Leadership Without Losing Your Soul, May 9, 2022, MP3 audio,
   31:43. https://letsgrowleaders.com/2022/05/06/the
   -earned-life-with-marshall-goldsmith/.

CHAPTER 32

1. Hyken, Shep. "ACA State of Customer Service and CX Survey."
   Shep Hyken Customer Service Research, March 2023. Accessed
   June 28, 2023. https://hyken.com/wp-content/uploads/2023
   /03/2023-ACA-Study.pdf.

Index

More Books by Karin and David

Courageous Cultures: How to Build Teams of Micro-Innovators, Problem Solvers, and Customer Advocates

"By following the guidance in this savvy book, you'll attract first-rate talent, serve your customers better, and liberate people to perform their best."

—Daniel H. Pink,
New York Times best-selling author of *When, Drive,* and *To Sell Is Human*

Winning Well: A Manager's Guide to Getting Results—Without Losing Your Soul

"*Winning Well* challenges the win-at-all-costs mentality, offering specific tools and techniques for managers to achieve lasting results while remaining a decent person."

—Adam Grant,
New York Times best-selling author of *Think Again* and *Originals*

About the Authors

Karin Hurt and **David Dye** help human-centered leaders find clarity in uncertainty, drive innovation, and achieve breakthrough results. As CEO and president of Let's Grow Leaders, they are known for practical tools and leadership development programs that stick.

Karin Hurt inspires courage, confidence, and innovation. A former Verizon Wireless executive with more than two decades of experience in sales, customer service, and human resources, she has a track record of growing leaders, building great cultures, and inspiring high-performance teams. She was named to *Inc.*'s list of 100 Great Leadership Speakers and is the host of the popular *Asking for a Friend* show.

David Dye helps leaders and teams achieve transformational results without sacrificing their humanity. As a former executive and elected official, he is known for practical leadership techniques you can use right away and growing leaders with the confidence and competence to thrive during turbulence and change. He's the host of the popular podcast *Leadership Without Losing Your Soul* and has recently released an inspiring book of personal essays, *Tomorrow Together: Essays of Hope, Healing, and Humanity*.

Karin and **David's** other books include *Courageous Cultures: How to Build Teams of Micro-Innovators, Problem Solvers, and*

Customer Advocates and *Winning Well: A Manager's Guide to Getting Results—Without Losing Your Soul.* Karin and David are dedicated to their philanthropic initiative, Winning Wells, which provides clean water wells to communities struggling with access to safe water throughout Southeast Asia.